MIDI *for* MUSICIANS

Buying, installing, and using today's
electronic music-making equipment

Brad Hill

a cappella books

Library of Congress Cataloging-in-Publication Data

Hill, Brad.
Midi for musicians : buying, installing, and using today's
electronic music-making equipment / Brad Hill. — 1st ed.
p.   cm.
Includes index.
ISBN 1-55652-221-5 : $14.95 (paper)
1. Midi (Standard)   2. Computer sound processing.
3. Musical instruments, Electronic.   I. Title.
MT723.H54   1994
784.19'0285'46—dc20   94-9133
CIP
MN

Published by a cappella books
an imprint of Chicago Review Press, Incorporated
814 North Franklin Street
Chicago, Illinois 60610

First edition

ISBN 1-55652-221-5

Printed in the United States of America
5 4 3 2 1

Contents

How to Use
This Book

You are holding a guidebook to the marvels and mysteries of modern music technology. It is part tutor, part workbook, part reference source, and part buyer's guide. Sections of this book may be useful to an accomplished user of digital instruments, but it is really written for the beginner and recent beginner—those who have either taken the first steps into the world of digital instruments or who are contemplating doing so. The book may be approached in different ways depending on your preference. If you learn by doing, you'll probably want to open first to section 3, "Putting It Together," a hands-on tutorial that will help you establish a friendly working relationship with any equipment you already own. On the other hand, you may want to have a more theoretical understanding of MIDI and how it connects musical devices. If so, sit in a comfortable chair and take enough time to read through the first two sections, after which you will be able to hold up your end of any conversation on the topic. Or, you may have been around the block once already; for you the last few sections will be of more interest, where you can look up a term in the glossary or be guided in your next purchase.

This is a book with a positive attitude. I believe MIDI represents a phenomenon of music technology comparable in its impact to the CD player, or the advent of written notation. If you are hovering at the doorstep of this new world—looking through the toy-store window, as it were—I say come on in. The toys may not be free, but they sure are fun.

I
THE BASICS

1
Making Music in a Digitized World

As rewarding as technology can be to a citizen of the modern world, it can also be frustrating and bewildering. Nowhere is this more apparent than with music, which until about a decade ago was distinctly nontechnological, at least from the player's viewpoint. It takes some technological skill to build a piano, but to begin playing one all you really need to know is how to sit down. There are those who think the piano is on the fast track to extinction, giving way with dinosaur-like suddenness to digitized, sampled surrogates. Unlikely as that may be, it shows how thumbnail-sized computer chips have already altered what is considered possible. The speed with which this has occurred is perhaps the most amazing aspect of our computerized society, and certainly a major reason why we are often out of breath in our attempts to keep up.

Many people aren't sure all the changes electronic chips have made possible are positive ones. Technology seems friendly enough when it unobtrusively makes our lives easier. The computer chip that runs the cruise control of a car; the circuits that keep the microwave from turning a mug of coffee into a puddle of sludge; the digital switching that routes telephone calls—it's easy to be glad for these conveniences because they ask little of us. They're easy to learn, easy to love.

The learning curve steepens a lot when computer technology is applied to musical instruments. However, learning to play an acoustic instrument (like a piano) has never been life's easiest challenge either. On the other hand, new music technology de-emphasizes the need for hard-won musical expertise. But the more musical experience you have, the more you stand to benefit from a partnership with digital technology.

These two facts alone could explain why digital music-playing setups are becoming more common in living rooms and basements. Many people may feel too old to begin taking music lessons, an activity usually associated with childhood, but have no reluctance to approach musical devices that are relatively new to all of us. Others may be motivated, by the sheer fun of the new instruments, to develop the music skills they picked up earlier in life.

As we'll see, a huge, expanding variety of digital music tools now exist, something for every learning curve. And they are all tied together by a single facilitator, a unique item of technology that is enabling this revolution in recreational (and professional) music-making. No, it is not this book, but thanks for saying so. It's something much more high tech.

What Is MIDI?

When music technology moved into the 1980s, the digital revolution had already begun. Keyboards with internal microprocessors had been introduced and become popular. Manufacturers began to experiment with interfaces that would transfer digital information among their own various devices. By the beginning of the decade, it dawned on the electronics industry that, if each manufacturer developed its own, proprietary interface, it would not be beneficial to the growth of the entire industry, and it would ultimately prove frustrating to musicians. In a world where consumer-friendly standardization is evidently a trickier challenge than sending a robot to Mars, an agreement to create a standard interface for all equipment might have seemed to be a pipe dream. However, by 1983, the agreement had been completed, documented, implemented, and named: The Musical Instrument Digital Interface, or MIDI, for short. Throughout the 1980s and into the 1990s, the MIDI specification (or the "MIDI spec," referring to the technical details defining how it works) has been augmented occasionally with useful features, but it remains fundamentally the same as when it was introduced.

That's the history of MIDI in a nutshell. But, you may be asking, what *is* MIDI exactly, and what are its benefits? Here's a technical definition: MIDI is a software specification by which musical data is transferred among hardware devices. (We'll talk about musical data in the next chapter.) Here's another way of putting it: MIDI is like a universal translator through which keyboards can talk to each other, to computers, and to other digital-music devices. Or we can think of it as a language in its own right—a data dialect, if you will—that is understood by music synthesizers, sequencers, samplers, synchronizers, and many other devices. Thanks to MIDI, electronic instruments made by one company can now communicate with those made by another.

In the digital world, compatibility is always good news, at least from the consumer's point of view. This is MIDI's claim to fame: it brings instant compatibility to all kinds of digital music machines. This means the entire marketplace is open to enthusiasts, who are no longer bound to purchase equipment only from the company that made the first instrument they bought.

Some things that MIDI is (and isn't)

- It's not a skirt.
- It's not a French word.
- It's not something you buy. Unlike batteries, it's included in keyboards and other equipment.
- It is software, but you don't need a computer to run it. It's part of the software preloaded in digital instruments.
- It's not an acronym for Meandering Infants Demand Ice cream.
- It is an acronym for Musical Instrument Digital Interface.
- It's friendly. Really.

When digital instruments "talk" to each other, they are sharing musical information such as what note gets played, when it gets played, and how hard it gets played. (Unfortunately, MIDI cannot do anything about wrong notes that get played.) A more thorough description of this digital gossip will be given in the next chapter; suffice it to say that this interconnection among instruments allows us to assemble virtual desktop orchestras, giving us musical power unimagined (by most people) just fifteen years ago. Just as word processing and desktop publishing have brought typesetting and printing into the home, so MIDI has brought the recording studio into countless homes around the world.

Aside from the technical benefits of industrywide compatibility, MIDI brings potential advantages that can best be described as "life-quality" benefits. MIDI recording opens the door to musical expression for those with little musical training or expertise. In this way, it can enhance creativity in people of all ages and backgrounds. It is possible, with the help of a basic MIDI system, to take the first educational steps in composition, arranging, instrumentation, multitrack recording, and sound design. Many people have discovered, almost inadvertently, the professional possibilities of becoming fluent in this technology, turning their MIDI expertise into semiprofessional or professional activities.

```
┌─────────────────────────────────────┐
│                  2                   │
│             ─────────                │
│            How Does                  │
│          MIDI Work?                  │
│                                      │
└─────────────────────────────────────┘
```

A suggestion: don't skip this chapter. You might think, by its name, that you're in for a technical treatise filled with undecipherable strings of numbers, charts, and diagrams, comprehensible only to those with computer expertise. Not so. We are not concerned here with how MIDI works from a programmer's viewpoint; this is the chapter where we will explore the nuts and bolts of MIDI from a user's perspective. These explanations will make the rest of the book more understandable for anyone relatively new to MIDI. And the other chapters refer to this one so often that by the end of the book you probably will have read it anyway; you might as well save time by absorbing it now. Painlessness is promised.

This chapter will refer to MIDI components that will be introduced in detail in section 2. It is not necessary to have a full understanding of these items just yet.

Musical Data

The most fundamental aspect of MIDI, and the most important to remember, is that it does not deal with musical sound at all; it only deals with musical data. This is so important, it's worth saying a few different ways. MIDI has no way of recording, transmitting, or editing the actual sound produced by a piano, an electronic keyboard, or any other instrument. Its purpose is to make music, to be sure, but only music produced by digital instruments that produce data when played. MIDI is not something you add to an instrument; it is an innate feature of modern digital instruments.

So what is musical data? For that matter, what is data? (Technically, we should say "What are data?," because a single piece of data is a datum. But nobody talks that way, and we won't either.) In the broadest sense, data is information. When we force our eyes open in the morning and glare at the clock, we are receiving visual data. When we hear the shower running and realize that there's a wait for the bathroom, we are perceiving aural data. When our noses tell us the toast has been burnt to a cinder, we are receiving olfactory data. On a basic level, anything we perceive is data.

We might say, therefore, that musical data includes the notes, phrases, and whole compositions of music that enter our ears. This data is transmitted in the form of sound waves that are "computed" by our ears and brains in a process called listening. There is also soundless musical data such as the printed notes on sheet music or the information encoded on a compact disc. We may eventually hear the result of this kind of data (by learning to play the sheet music or by playing the CD), but the data itself, unlike sound waves, carries no sound.

All of this is accurate, but not the definition we're looking for. Living as we do in the computer age, the word data, and therefore the term musical data, has more specific meanings. Data is electronically transmitted, binary information (sometimes referred to as "zeros and ones") that can be understood and processed by a computing device. Musical data is exactly the same stuff, but it is transmitted among musical computing devices, including keyboards, tone modules, drum machines, sequencers, and computers running music software. As we'll see, modern digital musical instruments are essentially specialized computers.

MIDI Events

Now we really get down to the nuts and bolts. We need to look inside the musical data and see how it is constructed. Not to worry: it's not necessary to get into bits and bytes. But this is where we'll discover why MIDI requires us to use different words for familiar musical concepts, and why, in order to have fun with MIDI, we need to think about music in a different way. For many people, the hardest aspect of MIDI is grasping the different vocabulary and the new approach to music that this system requires. This is what makes owner's manuals so cryptic to the uninitiated. Here's the bottom-line reassurance: it's worth it!

From now on, we'll be talking mostly about MIDI data, as opposed to musical data. They are really the same; MIDI data is musical data in a specific language, just as verbal data could be presented in different languages, such as English or German. MIDI, as we have discussed, is the language understood by digital instruments. As with a verbal language, the elements of the MIDI language can be organized into "words" and "sentences" that, when realized musically, become notes and phrases. The smallest item in our verbal language is the character (letter). The smallest item in the MIDI language is the "event." In each case these items usually have little meaning by themselves, and must be combined with other characters or events before a concept—either verbal or musical—can be completely formed.

MIDI events are generated whenever a MIDI instrument is played. The smallest musical statement that can be made is to play a single note. When you do this you hear that single note, but on the data level you have produced two MIDI events. First, a note-on event is generated when you press the key, followed by a note-off event when you release it. MIDI, like all digital languages, is very literal, and needs to account for everything. It does not assume, when the sound of a note fades out, that the note is off. It is only off when the key is released. So every note played on a MIDI instrument (it need not be a keyboard, though keyboards are the most common) requires a combination of these two events.

Note-on and note-off events are the most basic items of MIDI information, and they usually incorporate other data items that help form complete information "words." For example, which note is being played? In the MIDI scheme of things, notes are numbered according to where they are located on the piano keyboard. Middle C is referred to as C3, the C located one octave below that is C2, and so on. This information is included with the note-on and note-off events.

Velocity data is also part of the information packet. This can be a tricky concept to understand. Velocity means speed; in the context of traditional music, if we say that you are playing with great velocity, it means that you're playing at a fast tempo. The MIDI meaning of the term is completely different and has to do with volume, not speed. When you play an acoustic piano, the action of the keys and hammers is naturally touch-sensitive, which is to say that the harder you hit a key, the louder the resulting sound. This was a revolutionary breakthrough in music technology when the piano was invented, because previous keyboards, such as the harpsichord, were not sensitive in this way at all. (The original name for this exciting new instrument, in fact, was piano-forte, which is Italian for "soft-loud.") In the ensuing centuries, people have gotten used to the way a piano responds to the player's touch; digital instrument manufacturers were faced with the challenge of replicating that touch sensitivity in their instruments, which produce sound electronically, not mechanically. The answer has been to install sensors underneath the keys that measure how fast a key is being pushed down (in other words, how hard it's hit). This measurement is then translated into a certain volume of sound. Because it is the speed of the key that is being measured, the resulting data is known as "velocity information." Almost all keyboards are "velocity sensitive," and this information is included with the note-on and note-off events as well.

This, then, is the basic "word" of information needed to convey the sound of a single note: a note-on event, including key number (pitch) and velocity value (volume), followed by a note-off event, which also includes the key number. Actually, the note-off event includes a velocity value on some keyboards as well.

This may not seem to make sense. The note has already been struck, and its volume has already been established; why should key velocity enter the picture again? This extra item of information is called "release velocity," and measures how fast the key moves back into its off position. In these keyboards, the sounds can be programmed to fade out differently according to how fast the key is released. Letting the key up gradually might make the sound fade slowly, while removing the finger quickly can cause the sound to end abruptly.

Besides the basic note-on/note-off pair of events, there are other MIDI events that occur, and that can combine to form data "sentences." Between the note-on and the note-off, many things can happen. First of all, other notes can be played, creating their own packets of information "words." And within the duration of each note there are MIDI event possibilities. Aftertouch is one such possibility on some keyboards. Aftertouch events are generated by pressing down harder on the key after the note has sounded. This engages another sensor underneath the key, and the resulting MIDI information changes the sound in some way that has been preprogrammed. A typical use for aftertouch is to create vibrato, much as players of wind and string instruments, and singers, enliven the quality of their tones by causing them to waver slightly in pitch. Or aftertouch may be used to simply make the note louder. Whatever the sonic effect, there are two ways aftertouch is activated on keyboards. In the most basic way, any aftertouch applied to a single note affects all of the notes that are currently on. This is called "channel aftertouch." "Polyphonic" aftertouch enables each note to respond individually to its own aftertouch events, and to ignore the aftertouch generated on other keys. It is much more expressive, and relatively rare.

Most keyboards are equipped with a sustain foot pedal; pressing it will also add to the MIDI event sentence. This is modeled after the sustain pedal of a piano (the one on the far right), which lifts the felt dampers off the strings and allows them to vibrate—permitting the sound to sustain—until the pedal is released and the dampers are again resting on the strings. The use of this pedal on the piano is more subtle than merely lifting and lowering the dampers, however. Experienced players use shades of pedaling to create degrees of sustain in the sound; sometimes the dampers are just barely lifted off the strings, and this is called half-pedaling. With almost all digital keyboards, pedaling is a simple matter of engaging and disengaging an on/off pedal switch. (There are exceptions to this, and the difference in sensitivity lies within the keyboard, not with the pedal itself.) Therefore, when you depress the pedal to sustain a note, a "pedal-on" event is generated that allows you to remove your finger from the key without creating a note-off event; the sound is sustained. When you release the pedal, a pedal-off event ends the note.

You may have seen, on many keyboards, one or two wheel-like controllers to the left of the keys. These are the pitch-bend wheel and the modulation wheel, and they are also a source of MIDI events. The pitch-bend wheel "bends" a held note smoothly up or down in pitch. In its center, straight-up position, the note is heard at its natural pitch; pushing the wheel forward causes the note to swoop upward, while pulling the wheel toward you makes the note slide downward in pitch. On the data level, whenever the wheel is moved a stream of events is generated, representing a smooth curve of changing data values. When a note is bent upward and then down again, dozens of MIDI events are involved. Just bending upward by one half step would require many gradually incremented events. The modulation wheel works in the same way but usually controls some other aspect of a note's sound. As with the aftertouch feature, it typically adds vibrato, for example, or tremolo, which is a quick, fluttering variation in the volume of a note. Different keyboards allow the "mod wheel" to be programmed in different ways. (Those keyboards that contain aftertouch and a modulation wheel allow considerable expressive variation within a note's sound.)

The breath controller is another event-generator, though not a common one. This is a device with a mouthpiece at one end and a plug at the other that is inserted into a special jack on the back of the keyboard. The mouthpiece, naturally, is inserted into the player's mouth. Now, you can effect some expressive change in the sound by means of air pressure, as if the keyboard were a wind instrument such as a clarinet. Like the wheels, a continuous stream of data is generated, and the breath controller can change any number of qualities in the sound.

Of all these controllers, the ones that generate more than just on/off data (such as the wheels and the breath controller) are called continuous controllers, because they create a continuously changing stream of data, made up of individual MIDI events. All of these events, continuous or not, are also generated in nonkeyboard digital instruments such as MIDI saxophones and MIDI violins. But these instruments are not nearly as common, and are likely to have different controllers generating the events, because the method of playing them is so different.

MIDI events, and how to dress for them

MIDI events are very special. You may not think that a note-on, a note-off, or a pitch-bend is worth writing home about, but how often do you write home anyway?

The next time you attend a MIDI event, remember the following important facts:

- An event is not the same thing as a note. A note always contains at least two events: "on" and "off" (unless, of course, you hold a note down forever, which is considered impolite in dignified company).

- MIDI events are not sporting events. They are cultural events, like an opera or a stained-glass exhibition. Dress appropriately.

MIDI Cables and Ports

Now that we know what MIDI events are, the question arises, "What are they good for?" After all, a piano makes a sound when you push a key, and there are no MIDI events cluttering things up there. Couldn't an electronic keyboard be made to work without all this event business? In fact, weren't there electronic instruments before MIDI was invented?

Yes, there were, and a single keyboard can certainly produce sound without the need for MIDI events. The data a keyboard needs to communicate with itself—in other words, the communication between the keys and the circuits that actually produce sounds—needn't be generated in the MIDI language. In fact, in the pre-MIDI days, that was exactly the problem. Every keyboard spoke a different language. The great benefit of MIDI is that it enables digital instruments to communicate not with themselves but with each other. This is where MIDI events come in. They represent a language that every modern electronic instrument understands.

This communication is done through a special interfacing system that has two main components: the MIDI cable and the MIDI port. MIDI cables are sold in music stores, come in a variety of lengths, and have shielded five-pin connectors at each end; they plug into the MIDI ports that are located on the back of the instrument. There are three kinds of MIDI ports (also called MIDI jacks): IN, OUT, and THRU. Almost all MIDI components have the IN and OUT jacks, but some are missing the THRU.

Each MIDI port has a specific function. The OUT jack automatically transmits any events that have been generated within that component, whether or not there is a MIDI cable plugged into it (though of course if there is no cable attached to it, the transmission doesn't go anywhere). The IN port receives MIDI data that is being transmitted through a cable plugged into it. The THRU jack has the specialized task of replicating any information that is coming through the IN jack, and transmitting it right back out, which it does regardless of the presence of a cable. The component is still able to respond to the incoming data, but it is simultaneously being circulated throughout the rest of the system by means of the THRU jack.

The whole value of MIDI compatibility is that different instruments, representing a wide palette of musical sounds, can be controlled or accessed by a single keyboard or other MIDI controller. A MIDI component can serve one of two roles in a system: either control (be a controller) or be controlled (be a slave). The controller generates the MIDI data and sends it; the slave receives the data and responds to it. (Perhaps an enlightened civilization shouldn't use terms like "controller" and "slave," even when referring to its machines, but we'll stick with the status quo for now.) Some components, such as tone modules, have no controller capabilities and must by definition be slaved to a controller in order to operate.

In this way instruments can be connected into systems whose configurations vary greatly. A two-keyboard system is possible, wherein each keyboard both controls and is slaved to the other. Or a single keyboard can control a whole bank of tone modules. Sequencers can be integrated into the MIDI data flow to record a keyboard's controller events, and then they can be used to control the keyboard in turn by playing back those events. The sounds of several instruments under one keyboard's control can be combined to create a virtual orchestra of sound. And the possibilities for recording are even more dramatic.

Details on how to accomplish these setups, and descriptions of the types of components available, are forthcoming in following sections. For now, back to the nuts and bolts at hand.

MIDI Channels

A "channel" is another item of information associated with MIDI events. This is one of the most useful aspects of the MIDI language, the single feature that gives MIDI its orchestral power when recording. MIDI information is generated, transmitted, received, and processed within sixteen organizational subdivisions called channels. They work similarly to television or radio stations, except they have nothing to do with airwave frequencies. Any time you play an electronic keyboard you are (whether you know it or not) playing on a certain channel, on the data level. The sound that comes out is not necessarily affected, but every MIDI event is tagged with the channel that created that event. If a MIDI event were spelled out in English, this is what it might be: "The note F3 (the F above middle C) has been struck (note-on) with a velocity value of 94 (pretty hard) on MIDI channel 4."

MIDI channels are two-way. Data events are sent according to one of the channels, and they are received with an acknowledgment of that channel. As such, keyboards can easily change the TRANSMIT channel number and the RECEIVE channel as well.

Why is this so valuable? When using a sequencer, separating data into discrete channels allows for multitrack, multi-MIDI-channel recording, wherein complex compositions with many different instrumental parts can be built up track by track. The channels help keep all the parts straight, and automate the responses of the various components in the data chain. Let's say we have a keyboard controlling two tone modules (see Figure A). The keyboard is set to transmit channel 1. The first module is set to receive channel 5, and the second is prepared to receive channel 1. When the keyboard is played, MIDI events are transmitted through MIDI OUT to the first module. Because it is set only to acknowledge channel 5 data, no sound

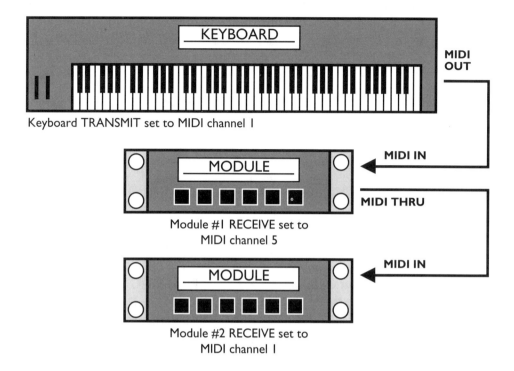

Figure A Using MIDI channels with two tone modules. In this configuration, module #1 does not make any sound. The data is passed on to module #2, which does produce tones, because there is a channel agreement between it and the keyboard.

is produced. Meanwhile, the data has been automatically retransmitted via the MIDI THRU port to the second module, which is prepared to receive data on this channel. It responds to the channel 1 data by sounding the notes being played on the keyboard. If this performance were being recorded into a data sequencer, we could then play (and record) another part with the keyboard set to transmit channel 5, which would enable the first module to get into the act. Then the sequencer could play back both parts, and both tone modules would be heard simultaneously, which would be impossible to do "live" with only one keyboard and two hands.

There is another important option when setting the RECEIVE channel. In addition to being able to set this to receive any single channel, there is an OMNI mode whereby all sixteen channels are received.[1] The OMNI mode is for keyboards

---

1 We should recognize an important distinction between "receiving" and "responding to." The truth is, any MIDI channel is always received, as long it is transmitted via a MIDI cable to the MIDI IN jack of the receiving component. The question is whether the data on that channel is ignored or responded to, and that depends on whether there is channel agreement.

and sound modules that can respond to different data streams, on different channels, simultaneously (most of them can). OMNI mode is typically used with a sequencer when recording a multipart piece. In this case, it is individual instrument sounds—not the keyboard or tone module as a whole—that are assigned to receive (respond to) their own MIDI channels. Now a single component can be an entire ensemble of instruments, each "playing" (through sequencer playback) its own part on its own MIDI channel.

Other MIDI Messages

Finally, we'll look at a couple of other useful commands that can be transmitted in the MIDI language.

In a keyboard or tone module, the instrument settings—that is, the preset sounds that come from the factory—are colloquially called "patches," and more formally referred to as "programs." A program, in this sense, is not to be confused with a software program used by a computer. It is a collection of settings within a digital instrument that produces a certain sound. When you change from one program to another, by changing the instrument setting, a "program change" command is generated as a MIDI event and automatically transmitted through the MIDI OUT jack. Any instrument that receives this command, if it is set to respond to the same MIDI channel the command was sent on, will also make a program change by switching instantly to a new patch.

It is important to remember that program changes are made on the basis of a numbered list of patches, and not by patch name or by the sound itself. This can make things a bit tricky. For example, your keyboard may have one hundred preset sound patches, numbered from 00 to 99. Patch number 00 might be a piano, and number 26 might be called pan flute. Let's say this keyboard is connected to a sound module that also has one hundred presets, and number 00 is also a piano sound, but number 26 is a patch called symphonic strings. If you change your keyboard sound from piano to pan flute, the program change command will make the same change in the tone module, but you will hear symphonic strings from the module. To complicate things further, not all numbering systems are the same. Some instruments begin numbering their patches with number 00, but others start at number 01, still others at number 11, and those that divide their patches into lettered banks begin with number A1. As far as the MIDI language is concerned, the first patch of one instrument is equivalent to the first patch of another, regardless of how they are numbered.

Anybody who explores MIDI will, before too long, come across the concept of system-exclusive data. This refers to the information generated by a single MIDI component to accomplish its internal tasks. It is exclusive to the system (that is, the keyboard or other instrument) that generated it, and though it can be transmitted over MIDI to another instrument of a different make and model, it will not be understood by that component. System-exclusive (often shortened to "sysex") data includes the internal settings required to create a keyboard's sounds, the order in which those sounds are stored in the instrument's patch banks, MIDI channel assignments, and global settings. It can be very useful to send all of this information through the MIDI connections to a storage device such as a computer disk. In the future, when you want to reset the keyboard's various parameters in the same way, it can be done automatically simply by having the keyboard receive that particular sysex data packet (this process is called a "sysex dump"). It is like storing a "registration" on an organ, except the information is even more detailed.

II
PIECES OF
THE PUZZLE

3
Keyboards

Of all the varied forms of MIDI equipment, by far the most common is the keyboard. It is usually your first acquisition in building a MIDI system, and is the one item that is self-sufficient. A keyboard will play as soon as it is taken out of the box and plugged in, without the need for other modules or controllers. (True, you may need to hook it up to an amplifier if you want to hear anything.) If the keyboard has autoplay features, you may only have to push a single button to hear a fully orchestrated piece. Talk about self-sufficient!

Keyboards have become so popular, in fact, that a vast selection of instruments is now available for beginner and professional alike, ranging from inexpensive, almost toylike models to hugely expensive, computer-interfaced music-production systems. Between these two extremes exists a constantly evolving world of music technology that can be bewildering to the uninitiated. Because keyboards are the most common interface between the human player and the realm of MIDI, we will devote quite a bit of attention to them. This chapter takes a generic approach in discussing general characteristics and different types of keyboards. Chapter 8 examines keyboard workstations, a recent and popular phenomenon. Chapter 4 explores in more detail how keyboards actually work in common recording and playing situations. And section 5 discusses what to look for when shopping for keyboards and other MIDI components.

Basic Features

All digital keyboard instruments, regardless of type, share certain basic features. The first and most obvious similarity among all makes and models is that every keyboard has a keyboard, that is, a piano-style arrangement of white and black keys that, when pressed, make sounds. There will not necessarily be as many keys as on a piano, which has eighty-eight; many keyboards are limited to five octaves (sixty-one keys), and some strike a middle ground with seventy-six keys, which is about half an octave shorter than a piano at each end.

Another distinction involves the degree to which a keyboard action (i.e., the entire keyboard mechanism) is "weighted." If through some mechanical contrivance the keys can be made slightly more difficult to push down, the result will be an instrument with a playing "feel" that approximates that of a piano. A piano's keys offer some natural resistance due to the complex and heavy arrangement of parts that is set in motion when a key is pushed. A digital keyboard produces its sound by means of sensors and circuitry and has no need for heavy keys, except to simulate a piano's action. The result is a range of keyboard feels, from the unweighted plastic action of many synthesizers and home keyboards to the realistic (by piano standards) actions of heavily weighted digital pianos.

Another common feature found on keyboards (except for controllers, which we'll discuss later) is the ability to produce a variety of sounds. In some cases the selection might be rather bare, as with a digital piano that may offer settings only for piano, organ, and harpsichord. A synthesizer, at the other extreme, is unlimited in this respect thanks to its ability to synthesize new sounds. Most general-purpose keyboards are equipped with fifty to 100 preset instrument sounds. Digital pianos generally have fewer; this is due to the large amount of onboard memory required to store a good piano sound.

The sounds a keyboard produces can be of two basic types: synthesized and sampled. A synthesized sound is artificially created using envelope generators, filters, and other digital sound processors. The result, though often pleasing, usually does not resemble actual acoustic instruments. A sampled sound is a digital recording of an instrument (or any noise, for that matter) that is stored on a memory chip. Samples require more memory than synthesized sounds, but, because of their realism, they have become very popular, and hardly any of today's keyboards are without them. When a model relies exclusively on samples for its sounds it is sometimes called a sample-playback keyboard. This is not to be confused with a sampler, a specialized instrument that can record its own samples (see chapter 3 of this section).

The Keyboard Controller

Larger MIDI systems sometimes feature an unusual keyboard called a keyboard controller. It produces no sounds of its own, but it is a MIDI component and is used to access the sounds in other keyboards and tone modules. There are advantages to having a single, master controller be the only keyboard that you actually play,

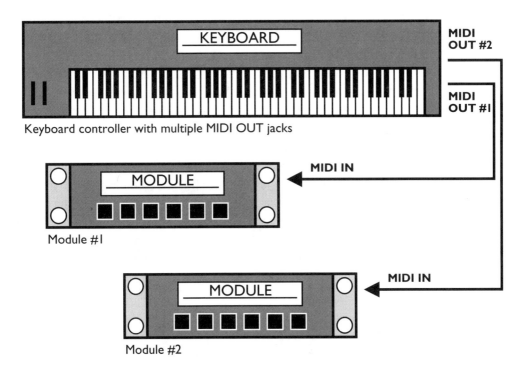

Keyboard controller with multiple MIDI OUT jacks

Module #1

Module #2

Figure A A master keyboard controller can address modules (or other keyboards) independently, with multiple MIDI OUT jacks. The two modules are not connected to each other.

though there may be other keyboards in the system whose sounds are used. Though soundless, keyboard controllers are rich in specialized features that help manage the MIDI data flow. They may have multiple MIDI OUT jacks (see Figure A). Different MIDI channels may be assigned to different sections of the keyboard. Usually controllers sport the full eighty-eight key range and weighted actions of a standard piano. This means they are quite heavy, and are often permanently installed in a recording studio. Some professional keyboardists—particularly those who work with complex MIDI setups on stage—require the extensive controller options and solid playing feel of a keyboard controller in a live environment as well.

Home and Professional Keyboards

It is not unusual for music stores to divide their keyboard inventory between two rooms: the main showroom and a back room whose door reads "professional keyboards." This does nothing to ease your confusion as a first-time shopper, not to mention your feelings of intimidation.

However, there is a reason for distinguishing between two types of keyboard, though recent technological and marketing developments are making it harder to draw the line between overlapping products. Traditionally, professional keyboards have been set apart on the basis of higher-quality sound and more powerful synthesis features. They generally have a less friendly user interface, making them harder to learn but more rewarding to use once learned. And, of course, this tone-shaping power and sonic excellence earn them generally higher prices.

Home keyboards have always been distinguished by less persuasive sound quality and less flexibility when it comes to altering the preset sounds or synthesizing new ones. The user interface usually offers many more buttons than on the pro models, so every function is visible and accessible. Autoplay features that provide bass lines, rhythms, and single-finger chords are also typically found on home keyboards. There is one distinguishing feature that has always divided the two categories, and perhaps always will: home keyboards have built-in speakers, and professional models don't. But speakers notwithstanding, there has been an influx of home keyboards on the market whose quality and features puts them on a par with less-expensive pro models. Sampling technology has dramatically improved the sound quality of home keyboards.

Digital Pianos

One type of keyboard began in the professional realm and has since become hugely popular as a home instrument. Digital pianos—also called sampled pianos—are electronic versions of acoustic pianos. Their memory chips contain recorded samples of grand pianos, as well as other instruments, and they are strictly sample-playback machines with no synthesis capabilities. Their actions tend to be weighted to further imitate a piano.

How can you tell a home digital piano from a professional model? Well, look for speakers and look at their general design. Home models are meant to reside in living rooms, in place of a real piano, and more effort is spent making the instrument attractive. A very sturdy, integrated stand is mandatory, whereas the professional units are like any other keyboard: a stand is optional, and the keyboard is designed to be put in a case for easy and frequent traveling. Some home models replace the ubiquitous black plastic sides with a simulated wood finish; some are built in the shape of a baby grand piano; one major manufacturer of digitals and acoustics even went so far as to house its digital piano in an acoustic wood cabinet, so that it looked (and almost sounded) like an upright piano.

The word "almost" must be emphasized in any discussion of how a digital piano sounds. Is it as good as an acoustic piano? Is it appropriate for someone who is beginning piano lessons? At present, digital pianos are an alternative to acoustic pianos, but not a replacement. The high-end models (and even some of the less expensive ones) sound impressive, to be sure; but the acoustics of a real piano are so complex and subtle as to be unattainable (at present) by the electronic counterpart.

Many people notice that digital pianos sound best when just one note is being played at a time. This is because the acoustic interplay that occurs in a traditional piano when many notes are played is missing; it may be hard to pinpoint just what is lacking, but something clearly is. Here's a simple experiment you can try in a store that sells both digitals and acoustics. Play a single note in the middle-to-lower range of an acoustic piano. Listen. Now depress the damper pedal and play the same note again. You should hear a subtly richer sound as the undamped strings vibrate in response to the struck note's sound waves. Now go to a digital piano and repeat the process. Enough said.

But digital pianos have definite advantages. For one, they require no maintenance—no tuning, regulating, or voicing—ever. Unlike the wood, felt, and metal components of an acoustic instrument, the circuit boards and plastic keys of the digitals are impervious to all but the most drastic extremes of climate and weather. They are generally less expensive than uprights, and certainly cost less than the grands from which their samples were recorded. They're more portable. And yes, they are acceptable instruments for beginners (as long as the keyboard is somewhat weighted), making them an attractive option for young families who cannot invest in a more expensive acoustic.

MIDI Acoustic Pianos

A relatively rare form of keyboard—the MIDI piano—combines the unequaled sound and feel of an acoustic piano with the orchestral power of MIDI. This may sound like another name for the digital piano, but in fact it is a *digitized* piano. Whereas a digital piano is an electronic instrument trying to sound acoustic, a MIDI piano is an acoustic instrument to which electronic components have been added. By installing sensors in the action that translate key movements into MIDI controller data, the piano can access sounds from other keyboards or tone modules. Of course, unlike a digital controller, the piano's own sound cannot be turned off, and because of this a MIDI piano is not an ideal controller for every studio or stage situation.

In recent years, a related phenomenon has emerged: the digital player piano. This represents the best of several worlds, and the future appears bright for these increasingly popular instruments. Traditional player pianos had an internal mechanism that would automatically "play" the keys; it was controlled by a long paper roll, into which holes were cut, so that individual notes would be activated. A MIDI player piano works in a similar manner but is "controlled" by MIDI data. As with the MIDI piano, the new players have sensors in the action so the piano can be used as a MIDI controller; but additionally, solenoids are installed that enable the piano's hammers and keys to respond to incoming data. This can be MIDI data from a keyboard or sequencer, or (in some models) the data can be stored on a computer disk that resides in a built-in disk drive. Thus equipped, a digital player piano can record a performance for posterity (perhaps a mixed blessing for most of us), then play it back at any time. If you grow weary of your own playing, libraries of prerecorded piano music disks are available for some brands.

If you already have a piano and are interested in giving it MIDI controller capabilities, retrofits are available from a number of specialized companies. These can transform your piano into either a MIDI piano or a digital player piano, but the retrofitting sometimes requires a fairly drastic surgical procedure involving the removal of a portion of the piano's keybed.

Voices and Polyphony

In the seventeenth century, choral music was polyphonic if it contained more than one part—or "voice"—performed simultaneously. In the modern keyboard world, the term carries the literal meaning of "many sounds." All digital keyboards are limited in the number of notes—voices—that can be sounded simultaneously. Early synthesizers could produce only one tone at a time and were therefore monophonic in nature. Typical ceilings of contemporary keyboards are six, eight, sixteen, twenty, twenty-four, or thirty-two voices, and this upper limit is called an instrument's polyphony. When an advertisement boasts that a keyboard is "sixteen-voice poly- phonic," we know that it will not sound more than sixteen notes at a time. Of course, very few people have seventeen fingers, and sixteen notes may seem ample for all occasions. But when working with a sequencer to record multipart music, it can quickly seem like a small allowance.

In fact, a keyboard's polyphony, and how the limit is implemented, is one of its most important features, even when playing without a sequencer. A piano, after all, often sustains many tones after they are played, thanks to the use of the damper pedal. If, as an example, you were to hold down the pedal and perform a sweeping glissando up all the white keys, the result would be a fifty-two note wave of discordant sound, each note sustaining until the pedal is released.

What would happen to the same glissando performed on a digital piano with sixteen-voice polyphony? The instrument's processors would allow the first sixteen notes to sound normally. As the seventeenth key is pressed, priority would be given to it as the most recent event, but some room would have to be made for this new note within the keyboard's capacity. This is done by shutting off a previous note's sustain as the new note begins to sound. (Which note gets turned off? Usually the first one played. Some keyboards, though, place an automatic priority on the lowest note played, so that no matter how complex the music becomes, the sound remains anchored in the bass.) This process would continue as your glissando moves up the keyboard, until at the end only the top sixteen notes would be sounding (or the top fifteen plus the lowest). Still discordant, but not nearly as full. Of course, there are

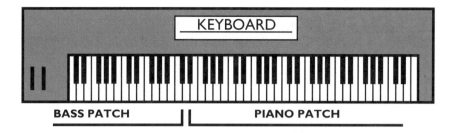

Figure B   Splitting a keyboard enables you to play two different sounds at once.

many more musical applications that require uninterrupted sustaining of many notes, so the greater the keyboard's polyphony, the better.

Multitimbrosity

While polyphony refers to the number of possible simultaneous notes, most present-day keyboards also feature the ability to sound more than one instrument setting at a time. When this is the case, a keyboard is called "multitimbral," meaning that different timbres can be played concurrently. There are a few different ways this can be accomplished.

The simplest implementation is called "layering," meaning that one instrument sound is layered onto another, and both are heard when the keyboard is played. In this way one might, for example, layer strings with piano for a lush, concertolike sound. Many digital pianos and home keyboards offer layering as an easily accessed option.

Another way to have two timbres available simultaneously is called "splitting." A split keyboard has one sound assigned to the lower portion and another to the upper range of keys (see Figure B). With this arrangement, you might hear an acoustic bass sample when you play with your left hand while the right-hand notes bring out a piano sound, enabling one person to sound like a duo. The point on the keyboard at which one timbre changes into the other is called the "split point," and is usually adjustable. The assignment of sounds is also under the user's control. Occasionally, home keyboards offer the option of allowing the player to assign a segment of the keyboard where the two sounds overlap, but this is neither common nor usually desirable.

The most powerful implementation of multitimbrosity involves assigning each of several timbres to its own MIDI channel (MIDI channels are introduced in chapter 2, and channel assignments are discussed thoroughly in chapter 14). Instruments with this capability became popular several years ago when multitrack sequencers became commonplace in home studios. Because a sequencer can record different musical parts, each on its own track, it became desirable to have keyboards that could play back more than one part—more than one instrument—at a time. Sequencing has become so popular that just about every professional-model keyboard made today is multitimbral to at least six parts. A single keyboard and a sequencer can now provide a virtual desktop orchestra—within the limits of the keyboard's polyphony.

Polyphony and multitimbrosity are easy to confuse. Polyphony refers to notes (also called voices); multitimbrosity refers to sounds (or timbres). So a sixteen-voice polyphonic instrument is not necessarily a sixteen-part multitimbral instrument—in fact it is not necessarily multitimbral at all, if it is a home keyboard. Conversely, an eight-part multitimbral keyboard is probably not limited to eight-voice polyphony.

Keyboard Peripherals

Finally, a few words on keyboard accessories, some of which are necessary and not usually included with the keyboard.

First and foremost, all electronic keyboards need some form of electric power. Most home keyboards (except for digital pianos) and a few pro models have battery compartments, and will operate for several hours on battery power. Otherwise the keyboard needs to be plugged into a wall outlet. Surprisingly, a power cord is not always included with home keyboards, particularly those manufactured overseas that need power adapters.

A keyboard should always come equipped with its own sustain pedal, a light plastic on/off pedal that is placed on the floor and plugs into the back of the keyboard. Home digital pianos have more stable pedal assemblies incorporated into their stands. Professional synthesizers and sample-playback equipment may allow for additional pedals that control different functions, which are never included in the manufacturer's package.

Keyboard stands are usually optional equipment, with the exception of the home-model digital piano. Other accessories that are usually not included are MIDI cables, blank disks for keyboards that incorporate a built-in floppy disk drive, and library disks for those same instruments. More information on library disks is found in chapter 15, which discusses all kinds of third-party products.

4

Sequencers

Nothing has contributed to the MIDI revolution more than the evolution of the sequencer. Though this is true even in the professional world of commercial music production, sequencing has played an especially important role in the growth of MIDI in the home. When it comes to opening the world of music to someone who has never become skilled at playing an instrument, the sequencer is the heart of MIDI.

Now that we've established its importance as a cultural force, let's start at the beginning. What in the world is a sequencer?

A sequencer is a recorder. But although a sequencer is analogous to a tape recorder, the principles under which it operates are actually completely different. The main difference is that a sequencer doesn't record *sound* at all. It cannot be played into; it is impossible to attach a microphone to one. A sequencer records only MIDI data, typically transmitted from a keyboard or other MIDI controller. Additionally (and not surprisingly), a sequencer is also capable of playing back this recorded data, typically to a keyboard, tone module, or drum machine.

Although sequencers can be compared to tape recorders, it is not the typical stereo tape deck to which they bear the greatest resemblance. A standard cassette deck, for example, records onto two tracks that, when played back together, create a stereo sound. Usually, these two tracks (left and right) cannot be recorded separately, only as a stereo pair. In contrast, a multitrack tape recorder divides a single reel of tape into several tracks (commonly four, eight, sixteen, twenty-four, thirty-two, or forty-eight) that are accessible for recording independently of each other. With this arrangement, a musical ensemble can be recorded one instrument at a time, and single parts (each on its own track) can be erased and rerecorded without affecting any of the surrounding tracks. This is how professional music production is accomplished. Likewise, sequencers come in various multitrack configurations, ranging from two tracks to hundreds, and they are able to record data independently to each track. So a complete definition of a sequencer would be: a multitrack MIDI data recorder/playback machine.

Other chapters discuss how to connect a sequencer to a keyboard (chapter 11), how to shop for a sequencer (chapter 19), and how to make the most of the unique possibilities that sequencing offers (chapter 15). Here, we'll explore how MIDI recording works basically, and the characteristics of different types of sequencers.

General Features

On the most basic level, all sequencers share certain characteristics: the ability to record, playback, and edit MIDI data. Though they are MIDI components, they are not MIDI instruments, in that they cannot make any sound by themselves. They work only when connected to a MIDI instrument (usually a keyboard), which sends to a sequencer the data to be recorded and receives from the sequencer this data to be played back again. So when we say a sequencer is playing back a piece of music (which in MIDI-speak is called a "sequence"), it is really only playing the recorded data back to a keyboard that then reproduces the musical sounds.

Section 1 introduced the concept of MIDI events. An event is anything done on a MIDI instrument that either produces sound or changes it. Events are generated when the keys are played (and also when they are released), when the pedal is depressed (and released), when the pitch-bend wheel is used, and so on. It is these events, carried through the MIDI cables, that are recorded by sequencers. When a sequencer plays back, it is merely sending these events, which have been recorded exactly in the sequence that they were played, back across the MIDI cables. When the keyboard receives them, its internal operating system translates the data back into sound, and the music is played back exactly as recorded. All this happens so fast as to seem instantaneous.

Editing refers to corrections and other manipulations of the data after it has been recorded, and this can be accomplished completely within the sequencer. The keyboard is not needed during the editing process, except to hear the result of any changes made. (We'll take a detailed look at what kind of editing is possible a bit later.) It is this aspect of sequencing that has made it so popular with so many people, because it eliminates the need for advanced playing skill as a prerequisite to making pleasing recordings. Add to this the multichannel personality of MIDI, and desktop music production is a recreational option for just about everyone.

Hardware Sequencers

There are two categories of sequencer: hardware and software. Software versions are for use with computers. Hardware sequencers, also sometimes called stand-alone sequencers, are separate physical components contained in a box, usually small enough to sit on top of a keyboard or nearby. On the sequencer's top panel is an array of buttons that may bear some resemblance to the controls on a tape deck, various other controls, and a screen of some size and communicative ability. On the back of the unit can be found the MIDI jacks, and possibly cassette-interface, pedal (for foot-controlled starts and stops), and metronome output jacks. A sequencer may also have a built-in floppy disk drive for storing your sequences on computer disks.

Stand-alone sequencers are generally less powerful than their software equivalents. First of all, they don't usually offer as many tracks; commonly the number is between two and sixteen, although some models go higher. On the software side, by contrast, sixteen is minimal, and total tracks can reach into the hundreds. When it comes to editing, hardware sequencing is also generally a less powerful option, though there are some very advanced machines on the market, as well as some extremely elementary software. There is absolutely no comparison between hard and soft sequencing in the user interface; no front panel screen on a stand-alone unit can compare with a computer monitor for giving graphic information about tracks and editing functions.

On the positive side, there are definite advantages to hardware sequencers, particularly if you don't already have a computer. Though stand-alone units are not less expensive, on the whole, than even high-quality software, they are certainly more economical than buying a computer *and* the software. They are also much more portable, so they are in greater demand among professional keyboardists who use sequenced material in their stage shows. And—again for those without computer experience—the learning curve is less intimidating than if you had to become computer literate just to record a piece on a digital piano.

Software Sequencers

It's hard to think of a piece of software, which lives as a collection of zeros and ones on a slim computer disk, as a component in a hardware-intensive MIDI system. But, like a hardware recorder, a software sequencer can be the central component in a recording setup.

Sequencing software offers extremely flexible and detailed control over your recorded musical events, and the graphic capability to show you exactly what you're doing at all times. Upon bootup, the first thing you would probably see is the main tracking window. Most programs have several windows for editing in different ways, and each program is organized differently. But one constant is an environment that allows you to label your tracks, and also the transport controls for starting, stopping, rewinding, and so forth. Other windows display the actual data in ways that make it easy to find an event(s) after it has been recorded. Sometimes the notes can be displayed as actual musical notation, as if you were looking at a piece of sheet music. Another popular display style resembles an old-style player piano roll that scrolls across the screen from right to left, with the notes represented as black marks corresponding to a vertical representation of a keyboard on the far left. Still other windows might be dedicated to showing controller information such as aftertouch commands and pitch bends.

Like most other current programs for all computer platforms, pull-down menus are available that activate other windows, engage various editing functions, and save your sequence files to disk. Many menu controls, and especially the transport controls, are duplicated as keyboard commands. The mouse is used primarily to delineate (or highlight) parts of the sequence—groups of measures, groups of tracks, or clusters of notes—that will be subject to an editing command. In short, the software sequencer is very much like a word processor, except that the data is musical in nature, not verbal.

Recording

Section 3 contains step-by-step help with recording in various MIDI configurations. Let's look at the basics of how all sequencers, hard and soft, accomplish this feat.

Sequencers are designed to enable you to build up, track by track, multipart musical pieces. In order for this to work, the different parts of the musical data need to be separated somehow (besides merely being placed on different tracks) so that when the keyboard receives the data on playback the various parts will be sounded by the correct instrument settings. For this reason all MIDI data is classified according to one of sixteen MIDI channels. Each part you play is "on" a certain channel, and this channel information is recorded as part of every event the sequencer receives. Because you have prepared for the recording by assigning certain instrument settings of your keyboard to certain MIDI channels, everything remains sorted out through recording and playback (for more information, see chapter 11).

From a sequencer's viewpoint (assuming a machine can have a point of view), tracks and channels have nothing to do with each other. A part recorded on channel 16 does not need to be placed on track 16, and data on track 4 does not necessarily play back on MIDI channel 4. Most sequencers, in fact, allow you to combine data with different channels on the same track.

One of life's great mysteries explained

Well, maybe that's overstating it a bit. It's not as mysterious as the Egyptian pyramids, but it's slightly more mysterious than housetraining a thirsty puppy. And it can be darned confusing to the MIDI beginner.

We're talking about the difference between tracks and channels. They are similar in concept, but different in function.

Confused yet? Good. Confusion builds character.

It's doubly confusing, because the word "channel" has a slightly different meaning as a MIDI term than in analog recording.

But here's the main point to remember about tracks and channels: You record *on* tracks, *by means of* channels.

In a sound studio (a non-MIDI recording studio), a music track is played through a microphone and routed from there into a mixing board. Several microphones can be plugged into a mixer simultaneously, each in a separate channel. These channels are then routed to the tracks of a tape deck, and the sound is recorded.

Hey, keep your eye on the puppy.

MIDI channels serve the same purpose—separating sound sources for recording on different tracks—but they work entirely differently. It's not a physical separation, it's a data designation, a digital distinction, a decimal differentiation (OK, you get the picture). A MIDI part is always on a certain MIDI channel; the channel number is part of the digital description of each note of the part.

Less confused? Fine. We're making progress.

Here's the bottom line: channels separate parts for recording onto tracks. In a MIDI studio, channels and tracks are software (not hardware), and virtual (not physical) distinctions. The following ingenious, helpfully illustrative table is offered at no additional charge:

MIDI	ANALOG
(software) data channel	(hardware) mixer channel
(virtual) sequencer track	(physical) tape track

For goodness sake, put some newspaper down for the dog.

The simplest and most obvious way to record a part into a sequencer is to use it just like a tape recorder: press record and play. This is called "real-time" recording (or, to be totally technical, "real-time data entry"). For those who are confident in their playing ability, it is the fastest way to get a part onto a track. It has the further advantage of allowing you to hear any previously recorded tracks—in real time—as you are playing in the new part.

But it is certainly not the only way to record. The easiest way to get out of real time is simply to slow the tempo down by lowering the metronome setting. This slows down the speed of the sequence but, unlike the effect of slowing down a tape recording, leaves all the pitches intact. Remember what it sounded like when you inadvertently played a 45-rpm record at 33 rpm? In addition to being much slower, the sound was comically low and growly. Conversely, accidentally playing an LP at 45 rpm yielded amusingly frantic, high-pitched results. One of the simple joys of data recording is that changing the speed has no effect on the pitch. So one good way of recording a part that may be too difficult to play in real time is to slow down the sequence, slowly play in the part, then reset the metronome to hear what the part sounds like at full tempo.

Sometimes, though, having the sequence playing along at any speed makes you feel rushed, and this is where step entry comes in. Even for accomplished instrumentalists, there are occasions when it is preferable to place the notes on the track one by one without any reference to tempo. This is exactly what step entry does. You choose the note value, such as half notes or sixteenth notes, then use your keyboard to place them in the track at your own pace. Because the sequencer doesn't enter the note in its proper place until you have released it (not when you first press it), it is possible to step enter chords.

Real time, slower tempo, and step entry are the three ways of recording fresh tracks, but there are other more specialized record modes. One of these is called "punching in" and involves replacing a portion of an already-recorded track. You simply tell the sequencer exactly what the desired punch-in and punch-out points are (many sequencers require these points to be at the beginning of measures), back up a few measures, and activate RECORD while in punch-in mode. The sequence will automatically shift into record exactly at the punch-in point, and shift back into PLAY when it reaches the punch-out. You are left free to play whatever you want to replace the old portion, and you can engage this process at any tempo.

One other record mode is "overdubbing." Traditionally, overdubbing means simply adding another track to the parts that have already been recorded. That can be done with sequencing also, of course, but the overdub mode specifically means to add data to a track that already has data on it. Normally, when you activate RECORD for a track that has been recorded on, whatever data is there will be wiped off to make room for the new part coming in. Overdub mode (which is not found on all models) allows the preexisting data to remain as new information is added. This is useful to flesh out a part without changing it substantially.

Editing

Recording data is just the beginning of the sequencing process. While most sequencers perform recording tasks in essentially the same way, they differ significantly in the power and style with which they let you manipulate your data. Again, software has an edge in clarity and precision, but many of the hardware machines can tackle any editing job.

For many of us, the sequencer's ability to correct mistakes is by itself enough to validate the entire MIDI technology. When recording on tape, after all, a single clunker can ruin a whole recording, and it's back to square one. When sequencing, we are free to clunk away; mistakes can be repaired later. This is true, at least, for sequencers that allow alterations of individual notes; not all do. Less expensive models may allow modifications only to entire tracks or measures. But that can be quite useful as well. You can, for example, change the MIDI channel of a track's data, enabling you to hear the part played by a different instrument setting. Rhythmic inconsistencies can be smoothed out with an editing process called quantizing. (It is quantizing that, when overused, gives sequenced music a mechanized sound.) A track or a group of measures can be transposed up or down a certain number of notes; in fact, the whole sequence can be easily transposed to a new key.

With the sequencers that do incorporate more precise editing, you can reach into any part you've recorded and adjust the exact placement, pitch, duration, and volume of any note. Of course, your sequence is bound to contain other MIDI events that are not actual notes—pedal movements, program changes, pitch bends, and so on—that can usually be accessed and altered as well (more information about track-level, measure-level, and event-level editing can be found in chapters 15 and 19).

Saving

Finally, a sequencer can save a sequence to some external storage medium so you can erase the internal memory and begin a new piece of music. Software sequencers, because they are run on computers, simply use the computer's disk drives to save the piece to a floppy or a hard disk. Hardware sequencers have to fend for themselves; some come equipped with built-in floppy disk drives. Normally these are 3.5-inch drives, but a few use smaller "microfloppy" disks. Hardware units that don't include disk capability usually include a cassette-interface jack on the back that permits you to save your sequence data to a standard cassette tape. It is worth remembering that you are not recording music in this process, just data. If you play it back on a hi-fi system, expecting to hear your musical creation, your ears will be in for a surprise.

Tedious (but true) facts about MIDI channels and tracks

- There are sixteen MIDI channels.
- Every MIDI event occurs on a specific MIDI channel.
- The parts of a musical piece are played on separate MIDI channels and recorded to sequencer tracks.
- MIDI places no limit on the number of tracks available.
- Track numbers and channel numbers don't need to correspond.
- Usually, sequencers can record (or merge) more than one channel on any track.
- MIDI channels do not make a good pizza topping.

5

Tone Modules

MIDI is a great equalizer. Its purpose is to make all digital instruments compatible with each other. But compatible instruments are not necessarily identical instruments. Through MIDI, two keyboards can share controller information and access each other's patches, but they may be very different-sounding instruments. This is unlike the world of acoustic instruments, where one piano—or flute or violin—sounds basically like another. There is variation in tonal quality, of course, but any one of these instruments is instantly recognizable. Not so with electronic keyboards. A synthesizer will sound very unlike a sampler, though they are both keyboards, just as a digital piano bears little sonic resemblance to a MIDI organ. This is why MIDI instruments are known by their make and model number. As such, a Yamaha DX-7 and a Korg T1 are considered to be individual musical instruments, unrelated to each other except through MIDI data-sharing and by the fact that they look pretty much the same. This is also why MIDI enthusiasts sometimes collect so much equipment, and why they might seem to be duplicating their efforts. Why own three keyboards? Because each one offers a different palette of sounds.

Actually, it is a bit inconvenient to have multiple keyboards in a home studio. They take up room and require stands. Performing keyboardists may need several keyboards in their stage setups in order to change sounds quickly, without pushing any buttons, or so that two keyboards can be played simultaneously. But in a home system, or any MIDI recording setup where speedy access is not the point, where any one keyboard can play another's sound patches, it seems like multiple keyboards shouldn't be necessary. And they're not. A tone module has everything a keyboard has—except the keyboard. Tone modules are the answer to the sprawling MIDI studio, and they have advantages beyond their economy of space.

Basic Features

Most tone modules (also called expansion modules or tone generators) are associated with a specific keyboard, and contain the same sounds and many of the same features. They are basically the "brains" of a keyboard in a different package, one that offers no controller features (unless there is a sequencer on board, which some have). The tone module is controlled by a keyboard ("slaved to" it), and this can be any MIDI keyboard, not necessarily the model from which the module is derived. Some tone generators, in fact, are not derived from a specific keyboard; they are independently created instruments.

Tone modules look like boxes; they are much less glamorous in appearance than keyboards. Usually, the module is nineteen inches wide and is fitted with permanent side brackets that enable the unit to be mounted in a standard rack. Standard racks are all the same width, are available in traveling or furniture styles, and vary in height according to the number of rack spaces they need. A rack space is about an inch and three-quarters high, and most tone modules take up between one and four rack spaces.

On the front panel of the tone module are the data sliders, buttons, and LCD screen. The MIDI jacks, audio outputs, and other interfaces are on the back. Nothing is on the top, bottom, or sides, because rack-mounted units are nestled very closely with each other and the inner sides of the rack. Some tone modules are designed not to be racked, but to be placed on a flat surface. They may be small enough to be placed on top of a keyboard. There are companies that specialize in making rack attachments for these tabletop designs.

Typically, manufacturers will introduce a new keyboard first, and then release a module version of it sometime later, usually within a year. The delay may be frustrating for musicians who don't need another keyboard but are in the market for new sounds. However, one advantage to this marketing tactic is that the module might include improvements over the original keyboard. Occasionally it will happen the other way around—module first, followed by a keyboard.

The One-keyboard System

With the idea that multiple keyboards can be replaced by tone modules, we begin to see that an entire MIDI system can be built around a single keyboard. How far can this idea be extended? Is there a limit to how many tone modules can be slaved to one keyboard? In theory, no. However, there are practical limitations.

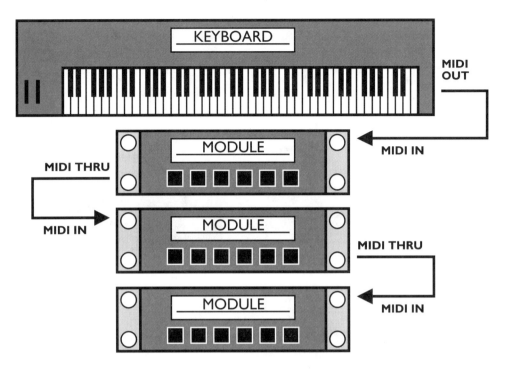

Figure A A typical data chain system. All the modules (or other keyboards, drum machines, etc.) receive data when the keyboard is played.

Multiple modules can be connected by their MIDI jacks in a chain (see Figure A). A cable runs from the MIDI OUT jack of the keyboard to the MIDI IN jack of the first module; then from the MIDI THRU of the module to the MIDI IN of the second module; and again from the MIDI THRU of the second module to the MIDI IN of the third; and so on indefinitely (see chapter 12 for step-by-step help in connecting modules). MIDI data moves so quickly that the sounding of a tone module from an external keyboard seems instantaneous, but the movement of controller information does take some time (milliseconds), and in the case of a very long chain of tone modules, a slightly audible delay could supposedly build up between pressing a key and hearing a sound. This limitation is really more theoretical than practical, especially because most multimodule owners use MIDI switchers to send controller data to all of their tone modules simultaneously (see chapter 7 of this section for more information on these switching devices).

A more practical limitation involves the MIDI channels: there are only sixteen of them. So, no matter how many tone modules are chained together, there are still only sixteen instrument assignments possible at any time. It can still be useful to have several modules with contrasting tonal palettes, as you may need five instruments from module A for one piece, while for another piece you might want to assign only instrument settings from module B.

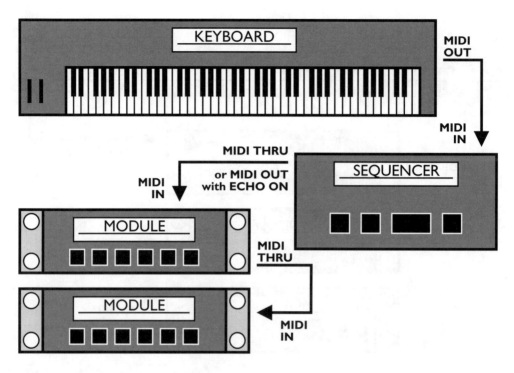

Figure B   A typical studio configuration, using a hardware sequencer in a data chain with two tone modules.

A typically expanded MIDI studio might consist of a single controlling keyboard, a sequencer or computer, and a rack of tone modules, each specializing in a different characteristic sound (see Figures B and C). The whole system would be connected either by a MIDI data chain or by a MIDI switcher (more on both methods later).

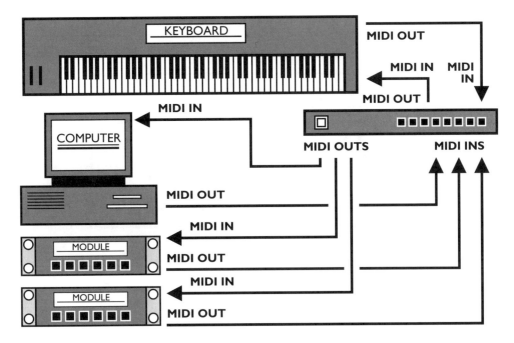

Figure C Another studio configuration showing the MIDI data flow when tone modules are used with a MIDI switcher. Using a computer for sequencing will be discussed in chapter 8 of this section.

6

Drum Machines

Drum and percussion sounds, as a separate group of electronically produced timbres, have always held a special place in electronic music. A drum set is different than any other musical instrument in that it is a collection of instruments played together that combine to make a whole. It makes sense, with the advent of digital music technology, that the drum machine, a special class of component, would be developed to incorporate the unique qualities of a drum set.

Drum machines are dedicated, surrogate, digital drum sets. Or you can think of them as digital drummers, because most of them are equipped with their own rhythm patterns.

Basic Features

The "traditional" drum machine comes with four basic features:

- An array of drum and percussion sounds.
- Pads for playing those sounds.
- A selection of onboard rhythm patterns.
- A pattern-based sequencer for recording your own rhythm patterns.

(It is strange to associate "tradition" with a relatively recent technological development, but drum machines have evolved so much that the distinction is necessary.)

The sounds in a drum machine are mostly digital samples of actual drum hits, cymbal crashes, conga slaps, and so on. They are stored in the machine's internal

ROM chips just as keyboard samples are. Instead of a keyboard though, drum machines offer raised pads on the front panel that can be tapped to produce the sounds. There are usually many more sounds on board than pads, so the sounds can be assigned to the pads in any configuration to make a custom drum kit. These kits can then be saved (usually) to a RAM memory slot for future use, freeing the pads to be reassigned. The traditional drum machine is not a rack-mounted unit, but a desktop one, enabling the user to get at the top of the box where the pads are.

The preset factory rhythm patterns make the traditional drum machine eminently useful right out of the box. These preset patterns are usually divided into banks of different styles, from rock to polka to swing to ethnic. The heart of the drum machine, though, is the sequencer that enables you to create custom patterns, and from these patterns create rhythm parts for whole songs. These sequencers are traditionally "pattern-based" as opposed to "linear": that is, they operate by repeating a pattern length over and over as you record one drum part after another until the rhythm part is complete. They are not linear like most stand-alone hardware and software sequencers, in which you record one track at a time of any length, and have access to the entire piece at once.

Newly created patterns are named and stored in memory, then used either by themselves to accompany a performance, or linked together in various ways to create songs either for performance or recording. These songs can then themselves be stored. Should memory limitations become a problem, many drum machines offer some means of externally storing your data—drum-kit settings, patterns, and songs. A floppy disk drive, RAM card slot, or cassette interface may be built in for storing the data.

As sampling technology has matured, drum machines have become more realistic sounding. Many acoustic percussion instruments are controlled in the same way that drum machines are—by striking something. This is unlike a violin, for example, which is controlled through applying pressure to a bow, a very different method than depressing a piano key. As a result, the violin is a difficult instrument to realistically capture through a keyboard-controlled sample. Because drums and keyboards (or drum machine pads) are controlled in pretty much the same way, percussion sounds are effectively rendered through MIDI, more so than many other instruments. High-quality drum machines can sound extremely persuasive.

In recent years drum machines have grown to include some other sounds that now must be considered part of their traditional arsenal. Bass samples are commonly found, so that in these machines the complete bass/drum rhythm section can be reproduced. Percussion sound effects that represent current trends at the time the machine was released are typical, as are miscellaneous effects that the designers thought might make an effective percussion element. Breaking glass, gunshots, grunts, scratching records, reverse cymbal samples, and other novelty sounds might find their way onto a drum machine's ROM chips.

Other parts of the traditional machine have evolved also. In particular, the pads are often velocity-sensitive, just like the keys of a keyboard, rendering the instrument far more expressive. Sequencers have also become more precise and sophisticated in their editing capabilities.

Recently, drum-machine technology has spun off in a direction that resulted in a different kind of instrument, one specifically suited to the MIDI recording studio. Percussion modules began to appear on the scene. These modules are similar in every respect to tone modules, except that they are dedicated to drum and percussion tones. These are rack-mounted components that have no pads. They are controlled from a MIDI keyboard, just like any other tone module. In many cases they also don't include sequencers, because they are primarily designed for use in studios that are already equipped with hardware or software sequencing. Because a portion of their internal memory is not taken up by recording functions, these models often contain more sound samples than a traditional drum machine.

Using a drum machine as a tone module involves a bit more setup than simply plugging it in and listening to preset patterns. Because the sounds are accessed by a keyboard, the keys in effect become drum pads for the drum machine. As such, they need to be assigned sounds; this is done by creating a keymap in which the drum machine's samples are "spread" across the keyboard in a user-determined arrangement. (Most percussion modules also come with some preset, keymapped "drum sets.") This is preferable to drum pads in a couple of ways. First of all, a five-octave keyboard has sixty-one keys, far more than the number of pads found on any drum machine, so the drum sets that can be created offer much more variety. Also, assuming the keyboard is velocity-sensitive, the drum sounds can be played with more expressiveness than from pads that lack sensitivity.

Once a percussion module is set up, percussion parts are recorded as part of a sequence in exactly the same way as melody and harmony parts. You simply play the parts one at a time, and if the sequencer has enough tracks, each part can remain separate from the others for easier editing. This is quite different from creating a rhythm in the pattern-based sequencer of a traditional drum machine. In that case, the track repeats over and over as new elements are added and automatically overdubbed, until the pattern has all the desired parts in place. There are ways of erasing specific parts, but it all (usually) remains on one track, and the process is somewhat more automated than with a linear sequencer. Recording in linear fashion is more open-ended and flexible, but requires a bit more work. Many linear sequencers, especially software ones, have some kind of pattern-mode ability, in which a single track can be looped over and over, and new parts automatically overdubbed onto existing ones, as on the traditional drum machine.

7
Samplers

The first synthesizers were very different from the keyboards we use today. They were large and unwieldy, could only play one note at a time (monophonic), and had no memory capacity for storing sound creations. They were "pure" synthesizers, in that they contained no preset sounds, and their only purpose was to synthesize new ones. As we approached the 1980s, more powerful and flexible keyboard synths were developed that gave the user much more variety and digital control over sound programming, plus presets and memory. In addition to being better, more convenient performance instruments, they simply sounded superior—though some people will say that something was lost in the transition from the older analog technology to the newer digital instruments. Certainly the newer keyboards sounded more realistic, at least when it came to emulating acoustic instruments. But it is very hard to capture the true sound of many acoustic instruments through the use of sound synthesis. The mathematically perfect waveforms used by these instruments differ drastically from the complex, "imperfect" waveforms generated by a hammer striking a string or a breath of air moving through the column of a flute.

As the desire for digital realism grew, many a musician must have thought, "If only there were a way of getting 'real-world' sound waves into a synthesizer." They didn't have long to wait. Sampling technology began appearing in the mid-1980s in keyboards that were no more expensive than earlier synthesizers. To say sampling was popular is an understatement. MIDI-controlled samplers and sample-playback instruments have changed the music industry, as they have changed home studios.

As discussed in chapter 3, a sample is a digital recording of a sound. It needn't be the sound of a musical instrument, although that is the most common application. This recorded sound (waveform) is then stored on a computer memory chip. The permanent waveform library of most modern keyboards is largely made up of samples. A sampler, on the other hand, can actually record the samples as well as store them. This is done through audio input jacks, into which microphones are connected.

How Sampling Works

Sampling means recording something digitally; by the same token, all digital recording is sampling. Usually, sampling refers to a short recording that can be used in keyboard playback, but literally speaking, even a complete symphony on a compact disc is a sample. To understand why it is called sampling, and how digital recording works, we should look quickly at what sound is.

Sound is the energy created by vibration. Usually this vibration happens too fast and too minutely to be visible to our eyes, although it is possible to watch a tuning fork vibrate. The vibration of a struck piano string is also easily visible, but we are not hearing the string directly; the sound that reaches our ears comes primarily from the vibration of the piano's soundboard as it responds to the movement of the string. At any rate, any physical vibration pushes against the air as it pulses back and forth. This creates waves of fluctuating air pressure, called sound waves. These sound waves create patterns of pressure against our eardrums, which results in the sensation of hearing.

Digital recording works by converting sound-wave patterns to digital information. The method for doing this is similar to the way a motion picture camera captures a moving image. The digital recorder takes audio "snapshots" of a moving waveform (a sound); by playing back this series of "pictures," the sound is replicated more or less accurately. Just how true to the original sound the recording is depends on a couple of important variables. One is the sample rate. This refers to the frequency of the snapshots, and is measured by the number of times per second that the sound wave is sampled. The higher that number is, the smoother and more realistic the playback of the sound will be. The standard sampling rate for compact disc recording is 44,100 samples per second (abbreviated to 44.1 kHz). Does that seem like a lot? Well, it is, especially when you consider that a motion picture camera only needs to shoot thirty frames per second to satisfy our visual expectations completely. The other important variable is the bit rate, which indicates how many bits of information are stored with each sample (snapshot). So while the sample rate determines the number of snapshots, the bit rate determines the quality of each one (see Figure A).

As a recording is being made, the digital information can be stored either on tape or on a memory chip. Samplers do not use tape; they put their samples in their

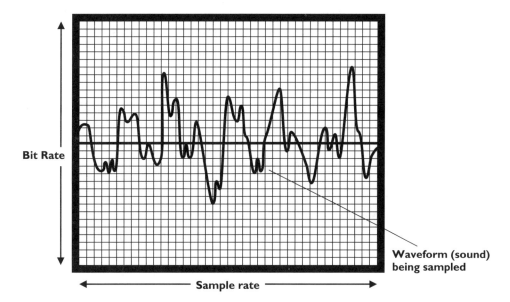

Bit Rate

Waveform (sound) being sampled

Sample rate

Figure A The digitization of a soundwave. Sounds are sampled at a certain "sample rate" (the number of samples per second), and a certain "bit rate" (the amount of data contained in each sample).

internal memory or send them directly to a built-in disk drive (either floppy or hard disk). Once that is done, the sample is available for playback from the keyboard; the instrument automatically transposes the sample to whatever note is being played.

How do I sample thee? Let me count the ways...

There are so many shades of meaning for the word sample, it's no wonder that a United Nations subcommittee has been established to sort them out. All right, maybe that's not exactly true, but it can certainly be confusing, even for non-diplomats.

On the smallest level, a sample is each one of the tiny, fast digital "snapshots" made by a digital recorder when recording a sound. When the sample rate is 44.1kHz, it means that 44,100 samples are being taken every second.

On the next level up, a sample is the whole result of all those snapshots, such as an entire instrument note recorded into a sampler. If this sample is five seconds long, it will contain oodles (that's the technical term) of tiny samples. (We'll let the U.N. committee do the actual counting.)

Up one more level. (Are you afraid of heights?) When an instrument is sampled, several notes are usually recorded, so that every part of the instrument's range is represented. This is called multisampling. In order to save time, and reduce the national debt, an entire multisample is usually called (you guessed it) a sample.

Top level. (Wow, look at that view.) Any digital recording, regardless of length or content, can be referred to as a sample. In this sense, an entire CD is a sample. This definition is more technical than colloquial, and you might think I'm being a nitpicking nuisance for pointing it out. We'll let the subcommittee decide.

General Features of Samplers

Like any other tone-generating device, a sampler can be either a keyboard or a tone module. In either case, there are characteristics common to all. The main identifying feature of all samplers is some kind of built-in recording capability. Recording original samples is accomplished through audio input jacks, into which can be plugged a microphone or the output of a mixer or an amplifier. Samplers perform four basic functions in their acquisition of waveforms: record, process, playback, storage.

When it comes to recording a sound, there are similarities and differences among samplers. Some can only record monaurally (in "mono"), while others support stereo sampling and have left and right stereo inputs. For some applications this may not make much difference, but to most people's ears stereo recording enlivens the sample and gives a spatial depth to the sound. The bit resolution can vary among samplers. The first consumer samplers were eight-bit devices, which is now considered to be on the low end of the scale. Twelve-bit sampling is a big improvement, and sixteen-bit represents CD-quality digitizing; higher resolutions are also found. To complicate matters, the bit resolution comes into play three different times in the sampling/playback process, and the number can change from one to another (specifics can be found in chapter 22). Most samplers offer variable sampling rates, which allow you to select a rate according to how much memory you'll allocate for a recording. Higher sampling rates require more memory and produce a better quality sample. In particular, high frequencies—such as those found in cymbals, for example—are represented better by using a high sample rate. Though the rate for compact discs is 44.1 kHz, many samplers go up to 48 kHz, and a few even higher.

Another recording variable is the number of multisamples allowed. The concept of multisamples is based on the fact that acoustic instruments have different tonal qualities in different parts of their pitch range. Because of this, samples don't always transpose very convincingly from one part of the keyboard to another; on the "real" instrument, it is not only the pitch that changes but the tone quality as well, whereas the sampler only transposes pitch. To get around this, most instrument samples are actually several samples—one every few notes of the instrument's range. This is

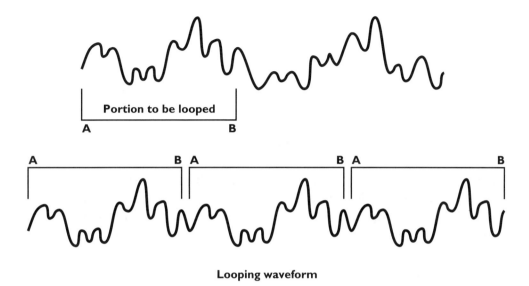

Portion to be looped

A   B

A   B A   B A   B

Looping waveform

Figure B A waveform can be looped (repeated) in its entirety, or, as in this illustration, a portion can be defined for looping.

called multisampling, and some samplers support this feature more flexibly than others.

The second basic function, processing, is a big area that includes functions that make the "raw" sample sound better and more persuasive. Probably the most important of these features is the looping function (see Figure B). Many instrument samples are too short for sustained tones; they may be no longer than a second or two, depending on memory constrictions. The solution is for the sampler to play back the waveform repeatedly and uninterruptedly as if it were on a tape loop. Because this is a digital process, and not a tape loop, it can be accomplished seamlessly. Even so, it is such an important part of the sampler's effectiveness that many different looping methods have been developed (see chapter 22). Aside from looping, a sampler's processing features can look about the same as any other keyboard's or synthesizer's, although they are not always as powerful. This makes sense, because a sampler's real power lies in the ability to record sound waves, not manipulate them. Still, most samplers are equipped with envelope generators, low-frequency oscillators (LFOs), filters, and other basic synthesis features (see chapter 14 for a more thorough description of these functions).

A special note should be made about digital signal processing (DSP), because DSP has a different meaning in a sampler than in a synthesizer. The DSP in a nonsampling keyboard refers to reverb, equalization (EQ), chorusing, delay, and other spatial effects that are applied to the sound. In a sampler, DSP refers to manipulation of the sampled waveform data, and includes processing functions by which the sample is spliced, truncated, compressed or expanded in time, merged with another sample, reversed, and so on. It does not merely add ambience to a sample as with other keyboards, it actually changes the sample's data.

Adventures in Sampling

When I bought my sampler, it came with thirty disks of prerecorded, customized samples. Good thing it did, because a sampler won't sound a note until a sample is loaded into it, and the last thing you want to do when you bring home a new keyboard is to spend half a day creating a sound for it to play. Still, after a while, you begin to crave some new sounds; in addition, the idea that a keyboard can play back any sound that can be recorded is very enticing. So I thought, anyway.

My first experiments were purely for my own entertainment. I sampled a Middle Eastern drum called a *dumbek*. This versatile little percussion instrument can make distinctly different tones depending on where and how it is hit. I divided the keyboard of the sampler into six regions, plugged a microphone into the input jack, and went to work. Recording each different drum "tone" separately, I assigned each one to a different region. Because each region contained several notes, I was able to produce even more tones by playing the different notes in a region, thereby transposing the original drum sound.

Next, I tried my luck with an unusual Bulgarian flute called a *kaval*. (I seem to collect esoteric instruments. Don't ask me why.) I wanted the sound of the kaval in some of my MIDI compositions, but even I must admit to how badly I play the thing. If I could get a good sample of it, though, I could simply play it on the keyboard. I knew that wind instruments need to be sampled many times throughout their pitch range if they are to sound effective; if a sample is transposed more than a few semitones up or down, the sound becomes artificial. Because I wanted to capture a range of two octaves, I divided that range into eight small keyboard regions of three semitones each. I played and recorded the bottom note of each region, and assigned the samples to the corresponding keyboard notes. This way, each sample only needed to be transposed upward by two semitones before the next sample was available to be played. It worked well. Now, with my fingers flying over the keyboard, I was an accomplished kaval player! (Well, not quite. But it's a lot easier than trying to learn how to play the real thing!)

For my next sampling project I turned my eye to my rack of tone modules. I had often put them all on the same MIDI channel, selected various patches from each of them, and played the whole rack at once like a one-man MIDI orchestra.

How convenient, I thought, if I could generate the same huge sound without tying up all my instruments at once. The solution: sample it.

This was going to be a bit tricky. The sampler I was using was finicky in one way: you could not use the keyboard to trigger the sound being sampled. In other words, it could not be used as a keyboard controller and a sampler simultaneously, and it was the only keyboard controller I had. The answer was to record the samples to tape first, then rerecord them from tape into the sampler. This is not ideal. It's simply less convenient and more time consuming. For another, recording on tape usually adds a little noise, which then becomes part of the sample. In this case, I divided the keyboard into ten regions, each defined by six semitones. This covered the entire five octave range of the keyboard. This meant that more transposing would be involved when the sample was played, but because the sample was an artificial sound (not an acoustic, natural one), that consideration became less important. After I had finished this, I could play that multimodule stack of sounds without using any of my modules, and could even stack more sounds with the sample, for a truly monstrous orchestra!

My next sampling needs were dictated by some soundtrack projects I was working on, which required that I be more experimental. Here's what I needed: the sound of a huge, heavy sword falling from a wall to the floor of a castle; the sound of mysterious knockings during a seance; and a sound effect that would represent the sheer terror of a man being driven mad by premonitions of someone rising from the dead. (All in a day's work for a MIDI producer!)

For the sword, I set up the sampler in my kitchen, which has a stone hearth under a wood stove. I tried dropping various items of metal kitchenware on this stone hearth, sampling all the while, until I found one that recorded with the necessary weight of a heavy sword. I think it was a cast iron skillet; whatever it was, my eardrums are still recovering from all the banging around. In the end, the sound I "played" for the soundtrack recording was several notes below the actual sampled pitch; I discovered that transposing it down added to the realism of the effect.

The seance scene was a bit easier. I knew it was supposed to sound like spirits knocking on the walls and windows of a room, so that's what I did. With a microphone set up, I banged like a madman on the walls and windows of my studio, which is fortunately in an old farmhouse that rattles easily. The samples came out beautifully. Again, by playing various keys above and below the assigned key of the sample, I was able to add variation to the effect, making it seem more natural.

On to the sound of terror. Here I let my imagination run freer. In the end, I recorded the sound of a screwdriver rubbed against the low strings of a grand piano with the sustain pedal depressed. This produced an interesting result, but my work was just beginning. I experimented with the programming parameters of the sampler, altering the raw sample beyond all recognition. What finally emerged, after changing the filter and envelope settings, was an indescribable sound that seemed to grate, scream, and choke all at once. It both underscored and enhanced the man's horrified hallucinations.

If these examples illustrate one thing, it's that sampling—though not always easy—gives play to the imagination like few other aspects of MIDI.

8
Workstations

If you were shopping for a stereo music system, you would have two basic choices. You could buy individual components, including a separate receiver, cassette deck, CD player, and speakers. Or you could choose an integrated system containing each of these components made by one company. The large, powerful "boom boxes" with built-in cassette and CD players are the most compact examples of integrated systems. Other packages are designed more appropriately for living rooms.

There are advantages to each approach. Shopping for components is more time-consuming, but enables you to select models that do one job very well. You may like the design of one company's tape decks, while another company makes a CD changer with exactly the features you want. Any audiophile will tell you that there can be a vast difference among speaker systems, and that, above all else, these should be carefully chosen. On the other hand, integrated all-in-one systems do a good basic job in every department, are convenient, and usually cost less than the components would retail for separately.

In the last few years, the same choice has been made available to home MIDI users. When MIDI was new (well, even newer than it still is) its entire value was based upon making different digital instrument components compatible with each other. This encouraged and established a modern music marketplace in which enthusiasts gleefully sought specialized units that would fill the gaps in their systems. The result has been music stores stuffed with all kinds of keyboards, sequencers, tone modules, drum machines, and samplers. As MIDI approached the 1990s, a new kind of machine arrived on the scene. To all outside appearances it was just another keyboard, but actually it was several MIDI components bundled together in keyboard form.

As usual in the inbred and highly competitive world of MIDI manufacturing, a few companies produced the first of these workstations more or less simultaneously. The main idea is to combine keyboard/sequencer/drum machine into a self-contained, music-production system. The instrument as a whole would represent one component in the MIDI data chain (assuming there were, or would be, other digital instruments in the system). Because the workstation was likely to cost no more than a good professional keyboard alone, it represented an attractive option for someone making a first MIDI purchase. The one machine had everything needed to begin playing, composing, and recording. In the meantime, workstations also have appealed to more experienced MIDI users, simply on the basis of sound quality. Even if you already have a sequencer, drum machine, and synthesizer, a workstation might offer the perfect solution of fresh instrument and drum samples to complement your current sound—and there's nothing to say you must use the onboard sequencer.

Basic Features

A keyboard workstation is first and foremost a keyboard, with all the basic keyboard attributes. A five-octave range is minimal, and the action is usually unweighted. There is a pedal, an LCD information screen, audio outputs, and the usual MIDI outputs and jacks. The addition of a sequencer makes a workstation what it is: a self-contained, portable recording studio. These integrated sequencers are usually not as full featured as stand-alone models, and certainly not as powerful as software recorders. Eight or sixteen tracks are typically made available, along with basic editing functions, such as, copying and deleting tracks, quantizing, step recording, inserting and erasing measures, punch-in recording, and multichannel recording. Sequencers are more prominently featured in some workstations as a powerful system component. For others, the sequencer is almost a second thought and is meant to be used only as a musical sketch pad.

Sometimes the sequencer is integrated with the workstation's internal system so that it behaves differently than an independent sequencer. In particular, the sequencer tracks may not be as flexible in recording MIDI channels. The tracks may be permanently connected (via the internal software) to certain MIDI channels, typically the channel that corresponds to the track number. This way, track 1 can only record MIDI channel 1, and if it receives data transmitted with a different channel number, it *changes* it to channel 1. Another method allows the user to assign various settings, including channel number and instrument sound, to each track before recording. This is more flexible, but still not as open as a sequencer that simply takes whatever channel it receives and records it. The difficulty with either of these systems is that one track cannot hold data transmitted on different MIDI channels (at least not without changing it all to the preassigned channel), so track merging is out of the question.

Many workstation sequencers support the kind of pattern recording that is popular with people who write pop-style songs. Popular song structure contains repeated sections representing verses, choruses, and bridges; pattern sequencers enable you to define, copy, edit, and exchange data as a section "pattern" that can extend over several tracks. This is more convenient than having to repeat several separate editing functions to accomplish the same thing.

This is not the same, however, as the kind of pattern recording found on most drum machines. Workstations include drum sections with the same sort of samples as are found on drum machines, but they work differently. It is the same difference that exists between a drum machine and a percussion module. Percussion modules lack the pads and sequencing capabilities of drum machines, as do most workstations. Drum machine sequencing involves repeating a defined number of measures over and over, building a rhythm pattern gradually by adding one part at a time, with each drum sound assigned to its own pad. In this way, the drum parts are being overdubbed continuously onto one track, which is all most drum machines have. Once a pattern is completed, it is strung together with other patterns to form a rhythm part for a whole song. Many workstation sequencers, even those with pattern editing across tracks, do not support this style of drum-machine recording of their percussion samples. In these machines drum sounds are treated just like the other sounds by the sequencer.

In line with their attempt to offer complete music production capability, workstations usually offer other features as well. A signal-processing section has become commonplace. This is where digital effects are generated (the next chapter focuses on MIDI peripherals and discusses digital signal processors). These effects include reverberation, digital delay (basically an echo), chorusing, and other sound enhancements. Most musicians feel digitally generated music sounds rather unnatural without such enhancements. In addition to the effects, most workstations include multiple audio outputs on the back panel. There will be a stereo pair of main outputs, which can be used by themselves, as well as some number of additional output jacks. When these are being used, any sound currently activated can be assigned an output. Each output can be plugged into its own mixer input channel (not to be confused with a MIDI channel, which is purely a data distinction), and its part controlled separately from the others. If you don't have enough input channels on your mixer for that, or if you don't have a mixer at all, most workstations will allow you to create a "pan" position for each sound within the two main stereo outputs. "Panning" refers to sweeping a sound from one side to the other in the stereo sound field. A sound could be assigned a position on the far left of the field, where it would be heard only out of the left speaker, the far right, or somewhere in the middle. Usually at least seven positions are offered between extreme left and right.

With all this self-sufficiency and production capability, you might think that a disk drive for storing created pieces of music would be a necessary feature. Surprisingly, this is not always included, despite the fact that many workstation owners are MIDI newcomers who have no computer or alternative storage facility. What some workstations offer instead are slots for RAM cards. These are credit-card-sized memory cards that can store banks of sounds, MIDI channel setups, and sequences. A single RAM card can cost one hundred times as much as a single floppy disk, and will probably not hold nearly as much information, and for this reason most serious users will arrange some kind of alternative storage (section 4, chapter 5 explores some of these options).

By the way, most workstations (and keyboards in general) that accept RAM cards also have slots for ROM cards, which work differently. RAM (Random Access Memory) stands for a kind of data storage that can be accessed flexibly. It can be retrieved, put back, and copied over; the card is empty when purchased and can be used, erased, and reused over and over. ROM (Read Only Memory) cards have information on them already (usually new instrument samples) and, while this information can be used, the card cannot be erased and reused. ROM cards are also expensive, but by adding new samples to the instrument's onboard library, the workstation's sonic palette is expanded substantially.

Other Hybrid Formats

A workstation without a keyboard would seem to go against the spirit of self-contained music production, because there would be no way of playing data into the sequencer, and indeed such modules are not considered workstations. But there are other integrations of separate components into a single instrument.

Just as keyboards are often repackaged as sound modules for those who don't need another keyboard but want the features and sounds that a particular keyboard offers, there are workstation-derived modules as well. In most cases they include everything the keyboard workstation includes, even the sequencer, despite the fact that most people who already have a keyboard, and thus purchase the rack-mounted module, probably already have a sequencer. Many musicians wish that manufacturers would eliminate the sequencer from the rack-mounted version and lower the price. The truth may be that it would cost more to redesign the circuitry than to simply import it as is from the keyboard.

At least one small, battery-powered instrument exists that must be called a workstation, though its functions are extremely limited. It has a rudimentary one-octave keyboard, several sound samples and programs, percussion sounds and preset rhythm patterns, a simple eight-track sequencer, and full MIDI capability. Its claim to fame is that it can fit into a purse or jacket pocket and is a great traveling companion. Songs can be sketched out while you're traveling on an airplane (earphones are used; it has no speakers), and later the data can be transferred to a more powerful sequencer for further work. We may see more of these compact units in the future, offering expanded features without sacrificing portability.

9
Peripherals

When putting together any system, the basics come first. In a MIDI system, the basics include keyboards, sequencers, tone modules, and computers. These items get the most attention, because they require the greatest investment. And, frankly, they're the most fun. But once the basics are taken care of, the marketplace is still crowded with secondary items. Some of these are necessary; others make MIDI easier or more entertaining. This is a similar process to assembling a stereo system. The basics include a receiver, an amplifier, a CD player, a tape deck, and speakers. Once you have those components and the cables to connect them, the system will work. But there are also powered FM antennas, remote controllers, equalizers, preamps, and other ancillary components that make the system work better or more conveniently.

MIDI Switchers and THRU Boxes

In previous chapters we've spoken of the MIDI data flow—the stream of digital information that links various components of a system. Like a real stream, it must sometimes be rerouted, dammed, or piped to areas where it is needed. Many MIDI systems implement a chain of connections from one component to another. A data loop is created that runs around the whole system and returns to the first controller instrument. For example, the data stream might begin from a master keyboard that sends its controlling data via MIDI OUT to a sequencer; the sequencer passes it on via MIDI THRU to a tone module; from there it continues to a drum machine; and

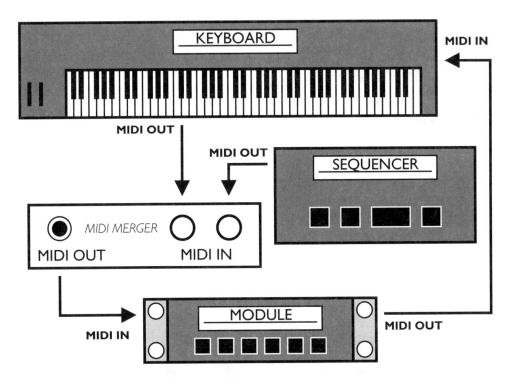

Figure A Using a MIDI merger. In this setup, LOCAL OFF should be set in the keyboard. This configuration is not for recording.

the drum machine sends it back to the keyboard. All the components are set internally to respond to the controller information in different ways, in some cases responding with sounds, and in others remaining silent. (Section 2 describes exactly how these setups work.)

Data chains work well at first, when a system is still relatively simple. If more components are added and the system becomes more complex, a centralized MIDI "switchboard" can be extremely useful and sometimes downright necessary. This is particularly true if you have more than one controller, as with systems that have two keyboards. (A sequencer is also a controller when it is playing back a piece.) It can also be useful when there are many slaves (tone modules and drum machines) that would create a long chain.

These switchboards are called MIDI switchers, and are basically boxes with MIDI jacks in them. The simplest version of such a device is a MIDI merger, which contains two MIDI INs and one MIDI OUT. Data that appears at the inputs is merged, and sent on its way in a single stream through the output. So, for example, if you are playing a keyboard part while your sequencer is playing prerecorded tracks, the MIDI information from each source can be merged and sent to the MIDI IN jack of a receiving tone module (see Figure A). MIDI mergers are simple devices

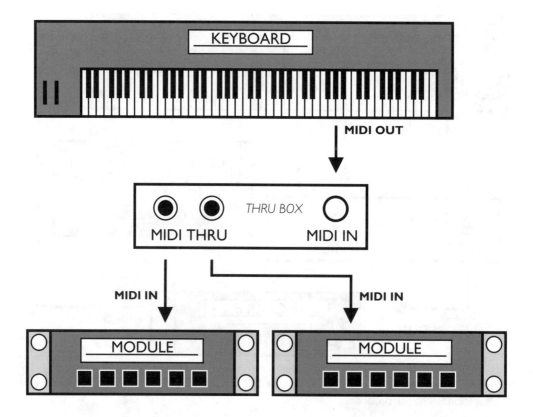

Figure B   Using a MIDI THRU box. A keyboard can control two (or more, depending on the THRU box) tone modules simultaneously, without setting up a data chain.

and often very compact, in some cases only a few inches square. They have been spotted in store sales for as little as ten dollars.

MIDI THRU boxes are also a simple kind of "switchboard." These devices have only one MIDI IN port and multiple MIDI OUTs. Information received at the MIDI IN is replicated and passed through the outputs. This enables you to control several slaves without setting up a chain (see Figure B). The controller (let's say it's a keyboard) sends its data to the input of the THRU box, where it is distributed to all the outputs. Those outputs are connected to the MIDI IN jacks of all the tone modules (or drum machines and other keyboard slaves). The MIDI THRU jacks of the tone modules can still be used to start data chains, if there are more tone modules than there are MIDI OUTs in the THRU box.

Full-featured MIDI switchers have both multiple inputs and outputs. This arrangement offers total flexibility in routing data. Information appearing at any input can be sent out any combination of outputs. This way, multiple controllers (say two keyboards and a sequencer) can be connected to the inputs, and as each one is used its data can be simultaneously sent to all the outputs that have tone generators connected to them. This kind of switcher is programmable, enabling you to determine how the data will be routed, and to save that routing configuration as a patch that can be called up easily from memory. In the above example, there would be one program (patch) for slaving the modules to one keyboard; another patch for slaving them to the second keyboard; and a third patch for slaving them to the sequencer.

Sometimes (quite often, actually) it is desirable to slave all the tone generators (modules, keyboards, and drum machines) to both a keyboard and sequencer. This way you can play a part on the keyboard (sending the data to the modules and the sequencer) while the sequencer is playing back the parts that have already been recorded on other tracks (sending its data to the modules and the keyboard). The modules need to receive data from both controllers (keyboard and sequencer), and the two controllers need to receive each other's data as well. To accomplish this the switcher needs to be able to merge data as well as route it. Some, but not all, switchers have the processing ability to do this, usually with any two inputs. The data streams from those two inputs are merged into one stream, and then routed to any combination of outputs. It's an important feature.

Speaking of processing power, many switchers offer some kind of data "massaging" as well. One example would be rechannelization, by means of which data received on a certain MIDI channel is automatically changed to another (perhaps the next one up) before it is sent to the outputs. Data filtering is also common; this enables you to eliminate certain types of MIDI controller information from the data stream. You might want to filter out continuous controllers such as aftertouch or pitch bends, if they are taking up too much of your sequencer memory. Or you could weed out the program change commands if they are disrupting the internal settings of your tone modules. Thinning a particularly thick data stream can also speed up the response time of your modules, though this is not a common problem.

MIDI switchers typically offer eight inputs and eight outputs, but the configuration varies. Sometimes there are fewer INs than OUTs, reflecting the fact that most systems have fewer controllers than slaves. Some units have as many as twenty of each, reflecting the fact that MIDI systems can be very complex beasts!

Disk Drives and Data Cards

As we've seen, many instruments have built-in disk drives for external storage of sound programs, multitimbral setups, and sequences. Many don't. Floppy disks offer the most convenient storage medium for this kind of information, and they are far and away the most cost-effective way to save your data. Keyboards and modules that lack disk drives sometimes have RAM card slots. RAM memory cards are convenient in that they are compact (though not all that much smaller than a 3½-inch floppy disk), and instruments can usually read data directly off them without having to load it into their internal RAM, saving a bit of time. Other than that, the advantages are all with disks. RAM cards are in most cases instrument specific, meaning that they cannot be usefully plugged into another model; they are much more expensive (typically $60–80, whereas a floppy disk costs about one dollar); and they can't hold as much information.

For all these reasons, a market has developed for external disk drives that can work for a variety of MIDI components. These devices are often rack mounted, almost always use standard 3½-inch computer disks, and can store sequences, patches, and system-exclusive information. They can save any information file that can be sent over MIDI. They have MIDI IN and OUT jacks, and are hooked up to the sending unit (or MIDI switcher) just like a tone module.

It should be noted that external disk drives are in no way to be confused with computers. They are strictly archiving devices and have no processing power whatsoever. However, they are flexible, can be used with many different instruments and sequencers, and in some cases offer file naming as a feature, so that keeping track of what you save is easy.

Alternate Controllers

Wondrous though sampling technology may be, and as realistic as modern samples are, it's still difficult to imitate the true sound of a nonkeyboard instrument from a keyboard. This is because of the differences in the way various instruments are played and their sounds controlled. For example, it is easy to accurately sample the tone of a single note played on a flute. But a flutist controls that tone with breath, and it is not at all easy to imitate the resulting nuances on a keyboard, which operates through touch. The same is true for a violin, a singer's voice, or a harmonica. Getting the tone is easy, but the performance style is a different matter.

The most realistic solution is to use the instrument itself, instead of a digital sample. But there are great advantages to putting the sound in the MIDI domain. In a recording situation, if the instrument's part (let's say a flute part) can be recorded as part of the sequence (as opposed to a "live" recording to tape), then it can be edited with the same precision as any other sequence track. This is such a production advantage that many composers and producers would rather sacrifice a bit of realism to accomplish it. In addition, of course, most nonprofessional MIDI users simply don't have the facilities to make live multitrack recordings. And we all know how hard it is to find a good flutist when you need one.

The result has been the development of MIDI controllers in nonkeyboard designs. These instruments are fully capable MIDI data controllers modeled on other acoustic instruments. The first alternate controllers were MIDI guitars. Actually, they were special attachments mounted under the strings of a regular electric guitar, much like a pickup, which converted the string vibrations into MIDI data and sent the information to a tone generator. Many guitar converters still work like this, although self-contained MIDI guitars have also become common. An early problem with these devices was the time delay required to convert the sound into data. This made playing fast passages difficult and disconcerting, because the converter could not track the notes as quickly as they were being played. This is still a concern, but tracking time has improved, as has the response time of the tone modules they are connected to.

There are self-contained MIDI controllers based on many other traditional acoustic instrument designs. In addition to guitars, there are MIDI trumpets, saxophones, violins, accordions, organs, and drums. These controllers don't usually produce any sounds by themselves. They have no built-in presets and are not acoustic instruments. In order to hear anything they must be connected through MIDI to a tone generator. Any module (or keyboard, for that matter) will work, but some of them come with their own specialized tone generator that contains sounds customized for that particular controller. These controllers enable a degree of expressive control impossible to obtain from a keyboard, since the MIDI data can now be affected by the breath, or the action of dragging a bow across strings.

Even though drum samples are realistically triggered from a keyboard, MIDI drum pads have become especially popular alternate controllers. A drum kit is an integrated collection of several different drums and cymbals, and playing them all as a single instrument is not possible to do effectively (at least not in "real time") from a keyboard. These MIDI drum kits vary in sophistication from simple lap units with six or eight pads to complete drum sets. The pads in these kits have no sound of their own but are connected through MIDI to a drum machine or a tone module's percussion samples.

MIDI controlling capability can also be added after the fact to an acoustic instrument. These MIDI retrofits turn actual acoustic instruments into data controllers, without taking away their natural sound. In this way pianos and accordions can "sound" like other instruments by accessing samples and synth patches in MIDI components.

Pitch-to-MIDI Converters

Another way to bring the control characteristics of acoustic instruments into the MIDI realm is with a device that translates any sound into MIDI data. Pitch-to-MIDI converters work a bit like samplers. They contain a microphone input, and they translate sound waves into digital information. However, their purpose is not to record that information for playback; it is to convert the analog waveform into a MIDI data stream and pass that information on to a MIDI tone generator or sequencer. When a tone module is used to receive the MIDI data, it produces notes just as if it were being played by a keyboard, and these notes will be heard virtually simultaneously. If the converter is MIDI'd directly to a sequencer, only the source acoustic instrument (or voice) will be heard; the data translation will be recorded as part of the sequence, and a MIDI sound program will have to be assigned to that track and channel later.

This makes it possible, for example, to play the saxophone part of a sequence on a real saxophone, with all the control nuances that an acoustic instrument affords, and then to assign a saxophone sample to the recorded MIDI track. There are two advantages to this process. First, the sample will sound better when controlled by a wind instrument than by a keyboard; second, the recorded notes are part of the MIDI sequence instead of on tape, and can be edited with the same precision and flexibility as the other tracks. It also makes possible such experiments as "singing" a flute part.

Synchronization Boxes

Synchronization boxes represent a somewhat more advanced use of MIDI, but a very useful one, and they are worth mentioning.

Very often, the digital world of MIDI recording and the analog world of tape recording need to coexist and interact. They are two different realms, with entirely separate formats, requirements, capabilities, and advantages, but it is possible, and necessary, to integrate them. One example would be scoring a MIDI soundtrack to a film; another would be a music project in which some of the tracks are MIDI-generated and some are live recordings of acoustic instruments (as is indeed the case on many popular albums). The difficulty is in locking together the timing when recording and playing back, so that when the tape is rolling and the sequencer is running, they are doing so in exact synchronization. This is accomplished by a "time code," which establishes a timing reference (like a metronome) that both the tape recorder and the sequencer can follow. There are several of these codes, each with its own special application.

The most common procedure is to record a time code onto one track of a multitrack tape. When the tape is played back, that code is sent to the sequencer, which understands the timing reference and slaves itself to it. In order for this to work, some kind of translating hardware box is needed that turns MIDI clocks into analog time code (to be recorded to the tape track), and then turns the time code back into MIDI clocks (to be fed back to the sequencer). Such devices have analog inputs and outputs, as well as MIDI IN and OUT jacks (see Figure C).

Here's how such a recording session would work. Let's say some sequence tracks have been prepared for a song. The drums have been recorded, as well as the bass and piano parts. These are all MIDI tracks triggering digital samples in tone modules and keyboards. The next track to be recorded is the lead vocal part. This, of course, will be a live track recorded to multitrack tape. First, the time code must be recorded

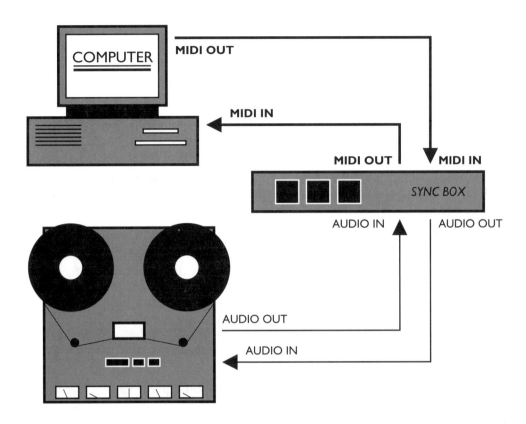

Figure C Using a synchronization box to record time code on tape. This way, a sequencer (either hardware or software) can be synchronized to live tape tracks. The sync box translates MIDI clocks to an audio tone, and back again.

to one track. To do this, the entire sequence is played back, with the sequencer or computer connected via MIDI to a synchronization box. As the MIDI clocks are received by this box, they are translated into analog time code and sent via the analog output to be recorded on a tape track. This done, the tape is rewound to the beginning of the time code, and the internal clock (metronome) of the sequencer is turned off. Now, when the tape is played back, the time code is sent to the analog input of the synchronization box, which translates it back to MIDI clocks and sends it via MIDI OUT to the sequencer/computer. The singer can now record the vocal tracks onto tape while hearing the prerecorded MIDI tracks, because the sequencer is "locked" (or slaved) to the tape.

Later, even after the live parts have been recorded, the MIDI sequence can be altered and edited, without losing its synchronization to the taped tracks. The sequencer's own metronome can be used (during which the taped tracks would not be heard), or it can remain slaved to tape (so that everything can be heard in context). It is sometimes more convenient to leave the taped parts out when working on the sequence, because moving from place to place in the song using the tape transport controls is relatively slow and inaccurate.

Do you really need to know about time codes?

Probably not. (Go ahead. Breathe a sigh of relief.) Most MIDI studios get by just fine without ever using time codes, or synchronization boxes. Sequences can be created, played back, and recorded to tape without ever thinking about time code (in fact, sequences rarely think about anything at all).

On the other hand, time code synchronization exists for a reason, and the day may come when you'll decide you want to use it. When that day comes, you'll be a better, wiser person, more able to cope with the curves and challenges of life.

The following conditions require learning more about time code, and acquiring a synchronization box:

1. You want to sync your sequence to live tracks recorded on multitrack tape.
2. You want to sync two sequences together on tape.
3. You want to score sequenced music to a film or video.
4. You want to impress friends with your knowledge and cool equipment.
5. You want to bore friends with your knowledge and cool equipment.

MIDI Interfaces

As mentioned in section 1, most computers require a MIDI interface before they can begin using MIDI software such as sequencers and patch editors. An interface can be as simple as a small device with MIDI jacks on it that plugs into one of the ports of the computer and makes it, in effect, MIDI-literate. In recent years, these products have evolved into more complex processors, bundled with additional useful features. Many include multiple MIDI IN and OUT jacks, so that they act as MIDI switchers in addition to being computer interfaces. Some even include time-code synchronization. Merging of MIDI data streams is sometimes possible, as well as MIDI event filtering. In short, many of the convenience options discussed in this chapter are now being packaged in some of these interfaces. In addition, the multiple MIDI jacks can expand (as long as your software supports this feature) the number of MIDI channels at your disposal. Instead of being limited to the sixteen channels defined by MIDI, you can expand your horizons by working with thirty-two, sixty-four, and in at least one case, ninety-six MIDI channels.

10
Computers

All of the components described in this section so far are, essentially, specialized computers. They create, organize, store, and play sounds, and manage the MIDI data flow, by means of digital-processing routines. A keyboard, in fact, can be described as a specialized computing platform with attached sound-generating hardware (if you were to be annoyingly overtechnical).

Since MIDI was developed in the early 1980s, when the digital revolution was well underway, it was natural for computers to get into the act. Computers don't naturally understand MIDI, but once they are "taught" the language, they are the perfect components around which to build a MIDI system, exactly because they are unspecialized processing tools that can accomplish many jobs equally well and relate productively with each of the more specialized components in the system.

Computers?! I hate computers!

Relax. Nobody said you had to get a computer. But why hate them? Computers are getting more prevalent all the time, and are easier to use than ever. They're fun, friendly, and can be trained to do the dishes. Well, fun and friendly, anyway. Besides, if you own a modern keyboard, you already have a computer. It just looks different than you expect.

Here are some of the advantages to getting a computer:

1. Computers offer much better, and more graphic, sequencing environments than stand-alone sequencers.
2. It's easier to program (create) new synthesizer sounds.
3. Storing sounds, whether created at home or purchased, is simpler.
4. A wide range of educational music programs are available.
5. Telecommunications (using a computer and a modem) with other MIDI enthusiasts around the world is possible.
6. Nonmusic computer software, such as word processing and accounting, is available.
7. You can play computer games (this is the main reason; all the others are just excuses).
8. You can be bothered night and day by friends, children, and grandchildren who want to play your computer games.

The Role of a Music Computer

The essential job of a computer in music is to serve as an intermediary between you, the user, and the MIDI data, to make your life easier. It is an interface, bridging the gap between the musician and the many thousands of data bits scurrying around. Its role is like that of a factory foreman, generally supervising more specialized workers. The computer's open-ended structure makes it ideal for this task, as do the graphic capability of the computer's monitor and the storage capacity of its disk drives.

Specifically, the computer's most popular MIDI application is replacing the stand-alone sequencer. Recording, editing, and playing back a multitrack composition is a complicated business, and in that role the processing and graphic power of a computer really shines. Software sequencing programs turn the computer into a sophisticated music-production environment similar to a professional multitrack recording studio.

Computers are also saviors when it comes to programming keyboards. There are two sides to programming: creating sounds and organizing/storing those sounds. A computer makes life much easier in both departments. To build a new sound program in a keyboard or tone module, many dozens of settings need to be adjusted (these are called "parameters"). The instrument's front-panel buttons and data-entry sliders can be used to do this, but the instrument's small LCD screen usually is only able to display one parameter at a time, and it is a gargantuan feat to keep in mind everything you're doing. The relatively large computer screen eases that problem considerably, and also can offer pictures of envelope shapes, waveforms, and other parameters that can simplify your task. Programmers who cut their teeth working on the front panels of their instruments and then switched to a computer wonder how they survived the former experience.

Software programs that help create sounds are called *editors*; those that help organize and store sounds are called *librarians*. The two functions are often combined into one program, which is then called an editor/librarian, or an ed/lib. These programs are usually written for specific keyboards or tone modules, and every program is created for a specific computer as well (more on this in a bit). So if you had a Macintosh computer and an XYZ-500 synthesizer for which you needed software support, you would need to look for "an ed/lib for the XYZ-500, written for the Macintosh." However, a few ed/libs are different. These are still written for a specific computer, like all software, but they can be used to program more than one instrument. So if you have two keyboards and three tone modules, you can use one of these so-called universal ed/libs to create and store sounds on all your instruments. Such a program is more expensive than a single-instrument ed/lib, but it might be the only editing software you'll ever need.

Computer Platforms

Not all computers are compatible with each other due to differences among operating systems. So what is an operating system, and wouldn't it be simpler if they were all the same?

Imagine for a moment someone who is very good at arithmetic. A bit of a genius, actually, who can multiply or divide lists of large numbers without recourse to pencil, paper, or computer. No matter what problem you give him, he is flawless. Though his ability seems superhuman, he is performing these mental feats from a basis we can all relate to. He calculates his answers using the base 10 number system we all use, and he speaks English, so he can understand the problems we pose and we can understand the answers. These are "systems" by which we all operate, and regardless of how different our friend may be from us in arithmetic talent, we will always be able to communicate within these systems.

A computer has special processing talents as well, but in this case we are one step further removed. We don't know its operating system—its native language— and it doesn't know any of ours. Software is the translator that can relate to both the computer's inner communication needs and ours. It is through software that we present the computer with problems to be solved, and through it that we receive the answers. The software can do its job primitively, sophisticatedly, with elegant simplicity, or with undue complication, but without it we are lost.

Even though the software is positioned as a liaison between the user and the computer, the computer's essential nature, as defined by its operating system, comes through every time we use it. Its personality may be refracted by software translation, but it is still evident, and this is in part why there are different operating systems. Different manufacturers think their system is easier to relate to, or prettier, or faster, or contains some other package of benefits that make working with it more productive and less stressful.

A computer's operating system is the foundation of abilities upon which it performs its processing tasks. This foundation is called the computer's "platform." You might think that with all the computer manufacturers around, there would be an impractical number of incompatible platforms. Actually, only a handful are prominent in the commercial marketplace: Apple Macintosh, Atari, IBM (MS-DOS), and Amiga.

In the MIDI marketplace, the most prevalent of these (at this writing, at least) is the Apple Macintosh. When MIDI emerged, the "Mac" had already established a formidable presence in homes and offices and a strong reputation for its friendly, graphically helpful operating system that made it easy to learn, even for the most compuphobic novice. Powerful MIDI software began to appear for the platform, and the Mac asserted its dominance in both professional and home studios.

This has been a disappointment for the Atari Corporation, which during this time was promoting a computer called the ST. The operating system was more similar to the Mac's than any other, and, from the user's point of view, the two computers seemed about the same. But the Ataris included one big advantage: they had MIDI jacks built into the back of the computer, along with the other standard interfaces, and thus a separate MIDI interface was rendered unnecessary. This seemed to signal Atari's foresight and commitment to MIDI computing. Although in Europe the Atari platform has gained wide acceptance, in the United States the computer enjoys only a small (but fiercely loyal) following.

The IBM platform offers the most complicated array of options. The operating system in this case is not installed permanently on the internal ROM memory chips, but must be loaded into the computer from a disk every time it is turned on. This is significant because it paves the way for development of new operating systems created by companies other than IBM. In fact, IBM deliberately opened the door to outside involvement in the platform by leaving every aspect of their hardware nonproprietary. This has resulted in a host of smaller hardware companies building and selling IBM "clones," computers that can accept an IBM operating system and run IBM-type programs, but are perhaps less expensive (and no doubt in a few cases less reliable). Although the range of hardware "cloning" is vast, with a crowded marketplace of choices, the development of operating systems has been dominated by the Microsoft Corp., whose disk operating system (its full name is MS-DOS) so overwhelmed the IBM world that the entire computing platform became known as the MS-DOS platform. More recently, Microsoft introduced a second operating system that is not meant to replace the first but to be stacked on top of it as an addition. Called Windows, its job is not only to add power to the platform, but—and perhaps primarily—to add a graphic friendliness that the platform had notoriously lacked. IBM, meanwhile, issued OS/2, meant to replace DOS. Competing operating systems are also making a more assertive stand for the attention of the IBM community, and this venerable platform continues to evolve.

Finally there is Amiga, which as a music platform enjoys pockets of popularity in different parts of the country. The Amiga has always been known as a preeminent platform for graphics work, and dedicated users also enjoy its unique natural ability to multitask. Multitasking refers to a computer's ability to run more than one program at a time; the user can then move effortlessly from one software application to another without dumping one and loading in another. This has since become a much more common feature on platforms other than the Amiga.

Which is the best computer to get for music applications? The purpose here is not to endorse but to balance the advantages and disadvantages of the different platforms. Atari is attractive because of its built-in MIDI capability, and because many of the models are amazingly cost effective. There are problems, though, created by the relatively small base of Atari users. Most software stores don't carry products for the platform, and finding a computer dealer who will repair (or sell, for that matter) the Atari line is difficult. Excellent software does exist, both for music and other applications (word processing, desktop publishing, games)—much of it of European or Canadian origin—but must be bought through the mail. You may wonder how you can know what you're getting if you can't see the software in a store before buying; many Atari users wonder also. If a prospective buyer is willing to become an active participant in the small but vibrant Atari community (the best source of information for Atari products), the powerful, inexpensive, MIDI-ready computer may make up for a definite lack of retail support for the platform.

At the other end of the spectrum, when it comes to retail support, is the Macintosh. It is one of the most popular home computers in the world for any application, musical or otherwise. It is friendly, powerful, prevalent among other MIDI users of all levels, and there is a wide selection of music software available for it. However, such an attractive package has traditionally commanded a high price tag, in addition to which must be added the cost of a MIDI interface. (Recently, Apple has introduced lower-priced versions of its machines.)

With the competitiveness among the various IBM clones, this platform offers a varied and cost-effective assortment of computer packages. The variety and easy availability of software is almost unbelievable, though not quite as spectacular when it comes to MIDI applications. As mentioned before, IBMs were never innovators in the art of user-friendliness, relying more on a keyboard-command-driven operating system than the intuitively easier point-and-click-with-a-mouse style of computing made popular by the Macintosh. (The typewriter part of a computer is called a keyboard, not to be confused with the musical instrument.) But the newer operating systems have taken huge steps in becoming more user friendly, though detractors point out that this is expensive friendliness (the operating system, remember, has to be bought separately from the computer, and without it the computer is useless), particularly because it merely (they would say) brings the user interface to a level already long attained by other platforms. Nevertheless, the hardware is sold everywhere, and there is a deep and diverse selection of software, especially business productivity programs.

The Amiga is well liked for its brilliant graphics and multitasking capabilities, as mentioned. It lacks a MIDI interface, and there is somewhat less MIDI software for the Amiga than for the other platforms.

Using a Computer with MIDI

Computers have become commonplace as MIDI components, and if you have a computer already, you might want to make it a MIDI-compatible device. When it comes to MIDI, most computers are illiterate; they need a translator. If a computer is going to be part of your MIDI setup, your first need is a MIDI interface. This is a small, separate piece of hardware that acts as a liaison between the computer and the digital instrument(s) (a more complete description of these devices is in chapter 7 of this section).

Of course, some kind of MIDI keyboard is a requirement, as are MIDI cables. With these, the keyboard and the computer are almost ready to talk to each other; software completes the equation. With these five elements—computer, software, interface, keyboard, and cables—a computer becomes an integrated part of a MIDI system.

III
PUTTING IT TOGETHER

11

Connecting a
Hardware Sequencer

In a home studio where the emphasis is on recording, the sequencer is the heart of the system. All sequencers have certain features in common, and these are defined and explained in chapter 4. Let's get one up and running.

Requirements

If you have a hardware sequencer (i.e., not computer software), this is what you need to record and play back music:

1. The sequencer, of course.
2. A multitimbral keyboard or other MIDI instrument (for simplicity's sake we'll assume it's a keyboard).
3. Two MIDI cables.

Basic Connections

This won't take long. There are only two steps (see Figure A):

1. Take one MIDI cable and connect the MIDI OUT jack of your keyboard to the MIDI IN jack of the sequencer. The sequencer can now record MIDI messages from the keyboard.
2. Take the other MIDI cable and connect the MIDI IN jack of the keyboard to the MIDI OUT jack of the sequencer. The keyboard can now respond to playback from the sequencer.

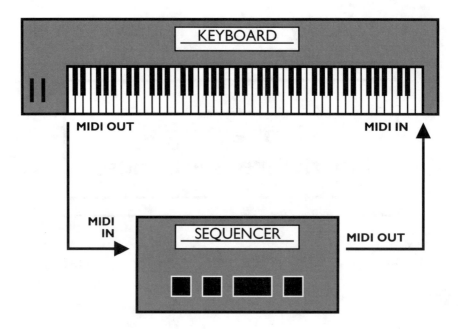

Figure A　The basic keyboard-sequencer setup.

Easy enough. You've achieved a basic MIDI recording system. Let's see if it works.

Recording a Track

First, select a sequencer track to record on. Refer to your owner's manual if the front panel buttons do not make this function obvious.

Second, choose a sound on your keyboard. Different keyboards refer to sounds as patches or programs. Any sound program will work, but we'll assume that you've chosen a piano patch.

Next, choose a MIDI channel to record with (MIDI channels are discussed in chapter 2). This is where things can be confusing at first. Any sound you choose to record with must be assigned to a MIDI channel (though on some keyboards the order is reversed: you choose a channel first and then assign a sound to it), and the keyboard must be set to transmit on that channel before you record.

?

Amazingly useful information about sounds, channels, and tracks

Here are a few things to remember, which may clarify this whole tangle of setting up a multichannel studio.

Sequencers are analogous to tape recorders and are often designed to emphasize the similarity. But it is important to remember one difference: sequencers do not record sound, they record MIDI data. (Sure, you know that. But the person in the back of the room is lagging behind.) When you press a key on your keyboard, a sequencer can record which key was pressed, how hard it was played, when it was released, how quickly it was released, whether any other controllers were used (such as the sustain pedal or pitch-bend wheel), and so forth. These are MIDI events, and it is the sequence of events that is recorded, not the sounds produced by the events.

This is crucial to understanding MIDI channels. (It's less useful when you're stuck in traffic and the car ahead of you overheats.) Every bit of MIDI information received by a sequencer is "tagged" with one of the sixteen available channels, and that channel data is recorded along with the rest of the event. So if a sequencer were muttering to itself as it recorded (bear with me on this), we might hear, "Well, middle C was pressed very hard on channel 9 on the first beat of measure three, and the sustain pedal was simultaneously depressed, also on channel 9." But this talkative sequencer would have no idea what sound was being heard during this event.

In order for this to work to our advantage, keyboards are equipped with the ability to transmit and receive different MIDI channels. Both of these settings need to be adjusted if you are to get the results that you expect. Most keyboards have an OMNI receive setting that should be chosen for sequencing purposes. With OMNI on, assign a different receive channel to each sound you want to use in your sequence. Then, whenever you change the transmit channel on your keyboard, you should hear the sound assigned to that channel, and you can record as if you were recording the sound itself.

Now, if your keyboard also talks to itself (c'mon, use your imagination), this is what we might hear as a sequence plays back: "Ah, I'm receiving some events on channel 3. Let's see, what sound is on that channel at the moment? Oh, electric organ. And now here come some events on channel 14, which is set to my acoustic bass sound. Boy, the two parts sound great together."

Tracks and channels are easily confused with each other, but they are entirely different. For one thing, there need not be any correspondence between channel number and track number. Also, a sequencer can have more than sixteen tracks (some software sequencing programs have hundreds). Finally, sequence tracks have no channel transmit or receive settings; they record whatever they get and play it back as such.

We'll assume your keyboard's piano sound has been assigned to channel I (though any channel would work) and your keyboard is transmitting on channel I as well. You're ready to record. Because this is just a test, don't bother with metronome or tempo settings. Just press the RECORD button of the sequencer (this should be obvious) and play something on the keyboard. It needn't be long or artistically sublime, though if sublimity comes naturally to you, all the better. When you're done, press the STOP button.

To hear what you have just recorded, press PLAY. If the playback seems inaccurate, or if you hear nothing, check the end of this chapter for some common problems and their solutions. Most problems are easily corrected oversights. If the playback proceeded correctly—well, you're up and running. For some, recording and playing back a single-track piano performance leaves nothing to be desired. But for many people the real fun lies in recording multiple tracks. Let's test that aspect of your system.

Recording a Second Track

The first step, naturally, is to select another track to record on, so that your first track is not erased.

Now select a new sound; let's make it a bass.

Once again you must select a MIDI channel for this sound. Any channel except the one assigned to the piano (channel 1) will work. Let's make it channel 2. And again you must be sure your keyboard is set to transmit the channel that corresponds to the sound you now want to record, in this case channel 2.

You're ready. Here's what should happen: When you press RECORD you will hear the piano part you recorded on the first track, and you will hear the bass part as you record it to the second track. Try it. Don't worry about playing "right notes," because we're still just testing the system. Most sequencers (but not all) will let you continue this second track beyond the end of the first, if you like. When you're done, press STOP.

Play it back from the beginning, and you should hear both tracks in a musically profound statement. Well, at any rate, you should hear both tracks.

A shockingly brief tutorial on how to manage sequencer tracks

The subject deserves a whole book. In fact, there is such a book: your owner's manual. With a little luck, reading it will be a useful exercise. Whether it is or not, experience and experimentation will be your best teachers. Then you can write your own book. In the meantime, here are some basic points, presented in the kind of immortal prose that makes grown men weep (whether in appreciation or frustration is not yet clear).

A sequencer may be equipped with two tracks or it may offer hundreds, but in principle all sequencers work in the same way. To make the most of your sequencer's power, it is important to think of your recorded parts as musical data—zeros and ones—that can be manipulated as easily as a calculator performs its computations. It may seem strange at first, but developing this habit of thought will make your results more satisfying and probably more musical. It will also make you less fun at parties.

In normal practice, you will record on only one track at a time. After each "take," you will need to either move the data to another track (using a "move" or "cut-and-paste" function) or move the record function to a different track. The point is to avoid erasing—or "overwriting"—the part you have just re-corded. Some sequencers will impetuously erase an entire track of data the moment you begin to record over it; others are less rash and will gradually overwrite data as you record, leaving the remainder of the track intact. Almost all sequencers contain a "punch-in" feature that allows a preselected segment of the track to be replaced with new material, while everything around the designated measures remains untouched even though you are in record mode.

One extremely useful feature common to all sequencers is the ability to merge two tracks of data. This is sometimes called "tracking down" or "mixing" data, and it actually expands the number of tracks at your disposal (see Figure B). As you approach the track limit of your sequencer, you can begin merging tracks, consolidating all your parts on a few tracks (or even one), thereby freeing tracks for new material.

This is augmented by the fact that, in most cases, sequencers will allow data from different MIDI channels to coexist on the same track. A related—and important—feature is not quite as common: the ability to extract data of one channel that has been merged with data of a different channel. Why is it important? Let's say that you've recorded several parts, and in order to free up track space you merge the piano and bass parts. Later you decide to change the

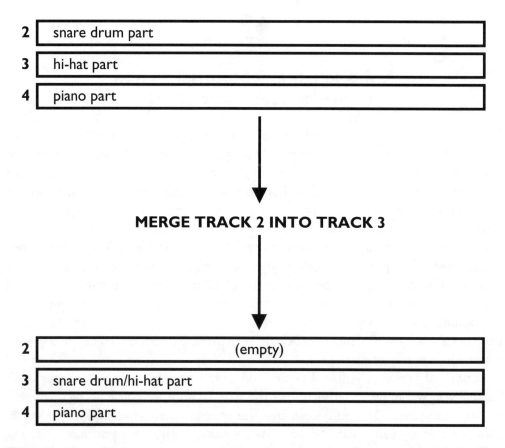

Figure B   Consolidating sequencer tracks through merging, thereby gaining extra tracks.

bass part across a sixteen-measure segment. If you can separate the two parts, there will be no problem deleting the now-offensive measures and replacing them. But if you can't, then any deletions will affect the piano part as well, and this may result in much teeth gnashing. For the sake of your dental well being, check for this feature before performing any merges.

Recording Multiple Tracks

This process can be repeated as often as you like, within the limits of your system. These limits are:

- The number of tracks in your sequencer.
- The number of parts your keyboard can respond to multitimbrally.
- Your keyboard's polyphony, or how many voices it can sound simultaneously.
- If these limits begin to restrict your creativity, you may be ready to upgrade.

It's not working!!

Stay calm. You've probably just done something you'll be embarrassed to admit later. I have a hundred personal examples of astonishing mental lapses, and I'm not going to confess a single one. (Of course, none of them is as humiliating as whatever mistake you just made.) My advice is to gloss over your trouble while it's happening, and then pretend it never existed after you've solved it; it works for me.

Problem

You've recorded a musical part to one track of your sequencer, but when you play it back you hear nothing. This is definitely aggravating. For your sake, I hope nobody else is in the room with you. If so, let her fix it.

Solution

There are several possible causes of this particular dilemma. Start with the obvious.

- Is the volume of your keyboard turned up?
- Check the connections of your MIDI cables. Make sure both cables are firmly inserted in the proper jacks: Keyboard OUT to Sequencer IN; Sequencer OUT to Keyboard IN. With a simple one-keyboard-and-sequencer setup, the THRU jack need not be used. (Wouldn't it be funny if you forgot about the MIDI cables entirely? No, I'm not going to admit that I ever did that.)
- Make sure your sequencer is playing back from the beginning of your recorded passage, and not simply proceeding from where you left off. Most sequencers will automatically "rewind" when you press STOP, unless set otherwise. (This is probably not the problem, and you should announce that with an air of glib authority to anyone who might be in the room.)
- Check the MIDI channel assignments. Remember that there must be a correspondence between the channel you transmitted (and recorded), and the channel(s) the keyboard is prepared to receive. Most keyboards have an OMNI receive setting, which you should assign right now if you're planning to record more than one part with more than one channel. This will prepare your keyboard to receive any and all channels the sequencer throws back at it.
- With your sequencer in edit mode, check to see if data was actually recorded. Consult your manual to see how to display an event list, or some

other confirmation that there is really something to be played back. (Imagine how you'll chuckle if the part never got recorded.) If not, the problem is with your connections or how the sequencer was operated; if so, the problem could still be the cable connections, or the MIDI channel assignments.

■ The perennial solution: Try again. Perhaps you pressed PLAY instead of RECORD. By the same token, when you play it back, make sure you're not pressing the RECORD button. (If it works after a second try, you can always pretend that you know why. Let your motto be, "Never look back.")

Problem

You've recorded a part, and when you play it back it sounds fine. But when you try to record a second track, you can no longer hear the first one. (Don't you hate it when *that* happens?)

Solution

You may be recording over the first track of data. Try recording on a different track or moving the first data to another track before recording the second part.

Also, when you change the channel transmit setting of your keyboard to record another part, you may be inadvertently changing the channel receive setting as well. OMNI receive is the best setting for sequencing.

Problem

You've hooked up your sequencer, and suddenly your keyboard sounds wrong. Notes are cutting each other off, and even single notes have a clipped sound. (What, you don't like it when notes cut each other off?)

Solution

Find the echo on/off setting in your sequencer and turn it off. When it is on, the sequencer sends MIDI events back to the keyboard as it receives them, so the keyboard's tone generators are receiving two events for every one you generate: one from the keyboard when you play a note, and one (almost simultaneously) from the sequencer. It's a kind of MIDI feedback loop, and can yield strange results. Another solution, if you want to leave the echo setting on, is to find the local on/off setting in your keyboard and turn it off. This way, the keyboard's tone generator will not receive MIDI events from its own keyboard.

Problem

You decide to merge two tracks. Let's say you have taken track 2, the trumpet part, and merged it with track 5, which contains a flute part. But now when you play back track 5, expecting to hear both parts, you only hear trumpet from track 2.

Solution

Well, maybe the flute part was no good anyway, and you're just as well off without it. OK, OK, keep reading.

Different sequencers have different names for track-editing functions, such as cut, copy, move, track down, merge, mix, clear, and so on. In this situation, the original data on track 5 was accidentally overwritten by—not merged with—the track 2 data. Read your owner's manual carefully to determine how your sequencer labels different editing functions.

12

Connecting Tone Modules to a Keyboard

For many people the greatest aspect of MIDI is its expandability. A keyboard may be purchased even with perceived shortcomings, justified by the understanding that they can be ameliorated later simply by adding an expansion module. Adding a tone module is a tempting way to enhance a keyboard, because it expands its range without sacrificing anything, as if new sounds had been installed on its internal chips. A tone module and a keyboard should work together as if they were one instrument. This is easy to imagine if you keep in mind that a keyboard alone is actually made up of two components: a keyboard controller and a tone generator. An additional tone module simply expands the sound-generating part of the keyboard.

Requirements

This is all you need to connect a single tone module to a keyboard:

1. A MIDI keyboard.
2. A MIDI tone module (alternately called a sound module, tone generator, or expansion module).
3. One MIDI cable (a second cable is optional, as we'll see).

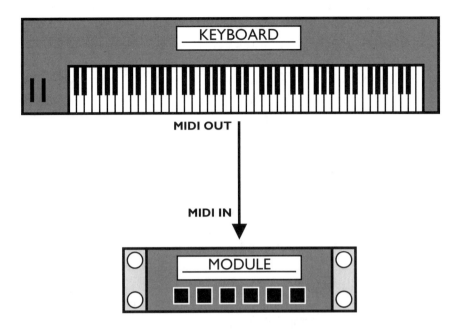

Figure A Connecting a tone module to a MIDI keyboard.

Basic Connections

This is very easy. There is only one step (see Figure A):

1. Connect the MIDI cable from the MIDI OUT jack on the back of the keyboard to the MIDI IN jack on the back of the tone module.

When plugging and unplugging MIDI cables (and any other interface cable, for that matter, whether on a MIDI instrument or a computer), the power should always be turned off.

Your keyboard has been expanded. Let's try it out.

Playing a Tone Module

Successful use of a tone module is largely a question of managing MIDI channels. You should be able to hear something right away just by playing the keyboard, because most MIDI components first turn on with channel 1 activated; if this is the case with your two units, then there will be channel agreement between them, and the module will respond when you press a key. The keyboard itself may be producing a tone also, and if you'd like to hear your new sound generator unsullied by any competing timbres, simply turn the keyboard volume down.

At this point it's a good idea to try all the preset instrument settings the module has to offer. Enjoy the sounds, get the hang of moving from one to another using the front-panel buttons (or sliders, or data-entry wheel), and explore each of the sounds for a while to get a feeling for what kind of playing style each responds to best. You are probably in the program bank, which is where the individual sound programs, or patches, are stored. (Different manufacturers have their own names for things, as defined in the owner's manual. The program bank may also be called the single bank or the internal bank.) There may also be a combination bank (sometimes called performance or multi—check that manual) where layered instrument ensembles are stored; go through these too.

You might want to explore other areas of the instrument such as the global settings and the MIDI functions, just to familiarize yourself with any terms you may encounter, even if you don't yet know what they mean. In short, tweak the front panel controls with reckless abandon. If you seem to be stuck somewhere and can't get the screen to show you the program bank where you started, simply turn the module off, wait a few seconds, and turn it on again. (The volume of any instrument—or of the amplifier or mixer it is connected to—should be turned down when the instrument is turned on and off.)

Presumably the volume of your keyboard is turned down at this stage, because you are uninterested in hearing the keyboard play along with the tone module. Nevertheless, while you're in the single program bank, try changing instrument settings on the keyboard, and keep your eye on the module's screen. It will probably jump to a different patch setting also, when you make the change. This is because it is receiving the program change command from the keyboard (program changes are discussed in chapter 14). Whenever you change from one program (sound) to another in any MIDI instrument, a program change command is sent through the MIDI OUT jack, and any instrument on the receiving end will change its program as well.

If the slaved module offers a larger number of patches than the controlling keyboard, they will not all be accessed by this method. For example, if your keyboard is a digital piano equipped with twelve instrument settings, and your module contains sixty-four preset sounds, you will be able to send program changes for only the first twelve of those sixty-four sounds. Some tone modules (and keyboards as well) contain program change maps that can be defined by the user so that any change command can select any patch. This way, if you particularly like the presets numbered 27, 34, and 59 in your module, you can set them to be activated when you press the first, second, and third instrument settings on your digital piano.

This is convenient, because the module can be located far from the keyboard, and patches can be selected by remote control. But the truth is it can be a severe nuisance as well. What if you simply want to change patches on the keyboard and leave the module's sound alone? There is a setting inside most tone modules that disables its response to program change commands. Look under Program Change in the manual; once you find the setting the screen will read "Receive Program

Change ON/OFF" or "Receive Program Change ENABLE/DISABLE." Disable it now; this will suit our purposes better. You may find a similar setting in the keyboard that will let you disable the sending of program changes.

Now turn the volume up on your keyboard. One of the satisfactions of adding an expansion module is layering the sounds of the two instruments. You may find that certain sounds on the keyboard that never appealed to you before are brought to life when combined with a tone from the module, and likewise the keyboard may enliven some of the module's less convincing tones. Now that you are free to change sounds on the keyboard without affecting the tone module, spend some time blending your expanded selection of timbres in every way possible. MIDI sounds best when sounds are effectively combined. Experimenting with this is fun, inspiring, and will open your ears to the possibilities of your system.

A Second Tone Module

The day may come when one tone module is not enough; that day may already have come. Manufacturers are constantly tempting us with new and dazzling sounds conveniently and compactly packaged. No justification is required for stockpiling tone modules; those of us who are accused of being addicted to MIDI admit it with pride.

Connecting the second module (and any future additions) is as easy as connecting the first. Simply take a MIDI cable and connect it from the MIDI THRU of the first tone module to the MIDI IN of the new one. MIDI THRU jacks duplicate all data received at the MIDI IN jack and pass it along unchanged to the next instrument in the chain (see Figure B).

You're ready. Now turn down the volume of your keyboard and the first tone module, and if everything is set to MIDI channel 1 you should hear your new sounds as you play the keyboard. To combine sounds from the different units, simply turn up the volume controls.

Setting a MIDI Channel

Actually, using the volume control to activate the tone module is not very practical. As much as possible, the idea is to control everything from the keyboard, where your hands are. Using the MIDI channels adds a degree of automation to your control of the tone modules.

Most tone modules can be set to respond to any of the sixteen MIDI channels. They will ignore any incoming data on a different channel. (That data will still be sent out the MIDI THRU jack, however; all data is, regardless of its MIDI channel.) There is also another channel setting called OMNI. When a tone generator is in OMNI mode it responds to all MIDI channels. This is the primary setting used in

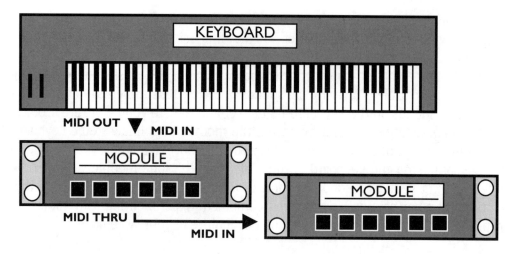

Figure B   Connecting a second tone module to a MIDI keyboard.

sequencing, when you want several instrument settings, each assigned to its own channel, to be available. Besides sequencing, OMNI can also be used when you want to have a particular sound from the tone module always layered with whatever sounds are being produced from other instruments on other channels.

For our purposes here, it is best not to be in OMNI mode. But you do want to assign each module to respond to its own MIDI channel. Look in the owner's manual to find out exactly how to accomplish this. The setting may be in a section (or "menu") of the tone module called "global" or "MIDI," and the actual parameter may read "RCV CH," which means "receive MIDI channel." (The word "receive," which is commonly used, is actually a bit misleading. All data, no matter what channel it's on, is always received if indeed it is sent. The MIDI channel setting determines whether that data will be responded to.) Set the first module to respond to channel 2, and the second module, if there is one, to channel 3. (We are saving channel 1 for the keyboard, which we'll deal with in a moment.) If you have more than two modules, you're probably not reading this primer, but nonetheless continue assigning each to its own channel.

Now, turn your attention to the keyboard. Because keyboards send controller data in addition to receiving data from other sources, they offer two kinds of channel setting: TRANSMIT and RECEIVE. Look in the user's manual for your keyboard and find how to set the TRANSMIT channel. In professional models with fairly large LCD screens, the parameter may be abbreviated to look something like XMIT CH, followed by a number indicating the channel. As with the modules, it's probably located in the MIDI or global sections. On home keyboards and digital pianos, you may simply be required to press a front-panel button (perhaps labeled MIDI) and one of the note keys at the same time. In this case, the manual will contain a map showing which keys on the keyboard correspond to the MIDI channel settings.

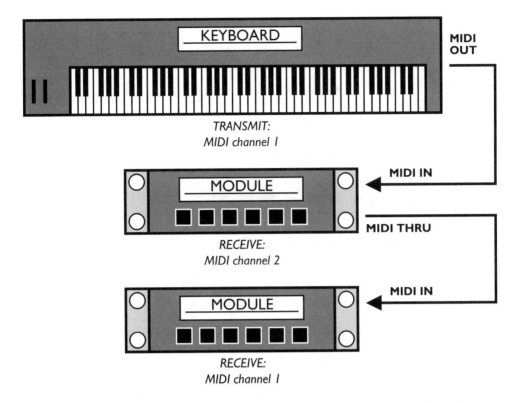

Figure C   Automating the response of tone modules by setting MIDI channels. In this illustration, the second module will play in response to the keyboard but not the first.

However it's done, by changing the TRANSMIT channel you can "turn on" your module(s) (see Figure C). When you switch to channel 2, the first module will sound the patch that is currently active. (Remember, you have not assigned a channel to a particular sound, you have assigned a channel to the whole instrument. You can change sounds freely without affecting the channel setting.) If you have a second module, switching to channel 3 will play it. At this point you are still controlling the keyboard's participation with the volume control. In order to fully automate the responses of modules and keyboard, so that the volume controls needn't be touched, a slightly different connection setup is required.

The Local Off Setup

Only one addition needs to be made to your current connections to fully automate the responses of your keyboard and external devices. You will need another MIDI cable. Connect this cable from the MIDI THRU of your last module (perhaps your only module) to the MIDI IN of the keyboard. If you visualize the MIDI connections now, you'll see that we have made a loop, beginning and ending with the keyboard

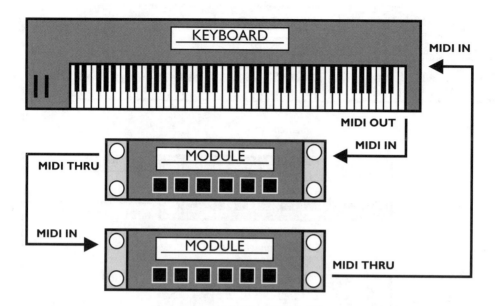

Figure D   The LOCAL OFF setup. The keyboard doesn't receive its own data until the end of the data chain.

(see Figure D). Data is generated by playing the keys and sent out of the MIDI OUT jack of the keyboard; it travels to the MIDI IN jack of the first module, continues on via the MIDI THRU jack to the MIDI IN of the second module (if there is one), goes out again by way of MIDI THRU and returns to the keyboard where it is received through MIDI IN.

This creates a somewhat schizophrenic situation as far as the keyboard is considered. Keep in mind that a keyboard is really two components: a controller (the actual keys) and a tone generator (see chapter 14 for more on this). The tone generator portion is now receiving data from the keys and, at virtually the same time, the same data that has traveled around the loop. This would be confusing for anybody, even a machine, and can lead to some unmusical results. Specifically, because every key is in effect being played twice at the same time, the notes tend to cancel each other out, leaving either a strangled-sounding tone or merely a click. Obviously this problem must be fixed. Because we've gone to the trouble of making this extra connection, thereby creating the situation, there must be a way to solve it short of ripping that extra MIDI cable out of the keyboard's MIDI IN jack.

The solution lies in disabling the other source of the doubled data: the keys themselves. We will, in effect, sever the connection between the keys and the internal tone generator of the keyboard. This is done with a setting called Local on/off, and this must be set to off. (Again, refer to your manual to discover how to make this setting. It is likely to be found in the same places as the channel assignments.) Local refers to the local keyboard, namely the one built into the keyboard instrument; turning it off disconnects it from the internal sounds, yet still enables it to send data through MIDI OUT. Now, when you press a key, the data flows out over the MIDI cables, through the modules and back to the keyboard, which then deals with the signal as if it were coming directly from the keys.

One more step. You now need to set the RECEIVE channel for the keyboard, just as you did for the module(s). (Get out that manual! It should be very similar to setting the TRANSMIT channel.) Set the keyboard to respond to channel 1, assuming your modules are set to channels 2, 3, and so on.

OK, you're there. This is a standard setup for controlling the participation of all the connected instruments without using volume controls. Here is how it works with two tone modules on line.

When the keyboard is set to transmit channel 1, data flows around the connection loop, returns to the keyboard and, because it is also set to receive channel 1, it sounds the notes you have played. The tone modules have disregarded the data because they are set to respond to different channels. When you change to transmit channel 2, the key data is likewise sent out over MIDI and sound is produced by the first module, because that is the only instrument whose receive channel agrees with the transmit channel. The data is passed on to the second module and back to the keyboard, but, because there is no agreement, the information is ignored and the instruments remain silent. Change to transmit channel 3, and only the second module will respond.

Keep in mind that once these channel assignments are made, they will hold until they are changed or until you turn the instrument's power off. Changing patch settings does not affect the channel settings.

To become fluent with this system, practice playing the keyboard while frequently changing the transmit channel setting.

Program Changes

As mentioned earlier, patches in a tone module can be changed remotely from the keyboard. We have disabled the PROGRAM CHANGE RECEIVE function in the modules. This needs to be enabled again if the modules are to receive their program changes from the keyboard.

It is important to remember that program-change information is just like any other MIDI data, in that it is sent, received, responded to, or ignored according to MIDI channel. This means you can target a patch change for just one module in your system.

A program change command is only a number; it has nothing to do with what a patch sounds like or what it is called. When you press the third instrument setting on a digital piano (let's say it is a harpsichord sound), it sends a piece of MIDI data to the module which says, in effect, "Change to the third patch in your program bank." That patch could be a flute, a drum set, a synthesized tone, or whatever the tone module happens to have stored in the third slot. This is why there are program change maps, so that you can instruct the tone module to automatically switch to patch #36, for example, when it receives a program change to #10.

All well and good. The difficulty is that you will always be changing the patch in the keyboard, even if you are not using channel 1, and even with local off. This is because local off only affects the keys, not the other front-panel buttons. When you change an instrument setting on channel 2 for your first module, the keyboard also changes sounds. You will need to switch back to channel 1 and reset your original keyboard patch. Not too convenient.

Why would anybody choose this method? Well, perhaps you will always want to be changing your patches in pairs—keyboard and module at the same time. In that case, arrange your program-change map to give you the desired tone module sound to be combined with each of the keyboard sounds you will be using.

One Big Instrument

The ideal MIDI system should function as one big instrument, and in this chapter we can begin to see how that works. The connections I've described do not represent the only way to arrange the MIDI data flow; many multimodule users employ MIDI switchers to replace the chaining system. There is no real advantage, however, unless a sequencer is being used. And that is the subject of the next chapter.

13
Using a Tone Module
with a Sequencer

There is a limit to what can be done with just two hands when you use MIDI to play "live" (even just for your own enjoyment). Of course, this limitation has existed for centuries, and it hasn't prevented the creation of some great music. But now, MIDI offers a better alternative. When a MIDI system is used for recording, the sequencer does the playing, and there is no limit to the possible complexity of your compositions.

It is in this environment that tone modules are most useful, and they are often the first addition to a simple keyboard/sequencer system. Be sure to purchase a multitimbral tone module, because multitimbrosity is essential for multipart recording. (Most expansion modules are indeed multitimbral.)

Requirements

To connect and integrate a single tone module into a sequencing system, the following is needed:

1. A sequencer (or computer with sequencing software and MIDI interface).

2. A keyboard.

3. A tone module (also called sound module, expansion module, or tone generator).

4. Three MIDI cables.

Connections

All the components need to be plugged in, naturally. But as always, when you're making your MIDI connections, leave the units turned off. Here's how to connect the MIDI cables (see Figures A and B):

1. Connect the keyboard's MIDI OUT to the sequencer's (or computer's) MIDI IN.
2. Connect the sequencer's (or computer's) MIDI OUT to the keyboard's MIDI IN. Those who have been using a keyboard and a sequencer have already made these first two connections.
3. Connect the keyboard's MIDI THRU to the sound module's MIDI IN.

As you probably know by now, the purpose of the MIDI THRU jack is to take any data received at MIDI IN and pass it along to the next component. However, most hardware sequencers and many computer MIDI interfaces do not have MIDI THRU jacks, so the MIDI OUT port must be used instead. A special setting needs to be made in the sequencer (or sequencing software); otherwise the MIDI OUT jack will not automatically pass along data received at MIDI IN. This setting may be called thru on/off or echo on/off (check your owner's manual). Setting it to ON changes the natural function of the MIDI OUT jack so that it behaves like a MIDI THRU jack. Make that setting now, if you are using a MIDI OUT jack from your sequencer/computer.

Next, you must change a crucial setting in your keyboard. With things set up as they are, the keyboard will be receiving every bit of data twice—once from itself, as it were, and again when the sequencer/computer sends the data back. (This is explained completely in the previous chapter; the reason for this setup will be clear shortly.) For now, it is important to prevent the keyboard's own keys from communicating directly with its internal tone generator, and this is accomplished with a setting known as local on/off. Find this with the help of your manual and set it to off.

Channel Assignments

If you have been using a multitimbral keyboard, you may know how to assign sounds to their own MIDI channels (or channels to sounds, depending on how the keyboard operates). All multitimbral tone modules offer some way of making these assignments as well. This is what makes the module multitimbral, because it can then respond to several channels simultaneously by sounding different instruments. How these assignments are made differs from model to model, and you will need to refer to your manual for details. There may be a section called Combination, Multi, or Performance in which every sound you want to use in the recording can be assigned not only a MIDI channel, but also a volume level, position in the stereo field, key

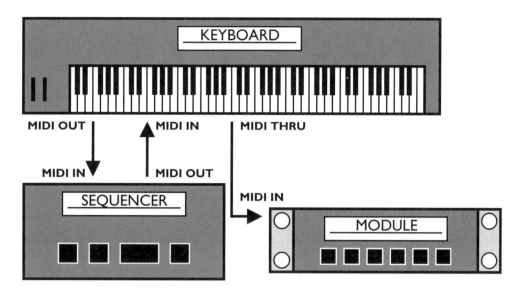

Figure A Adding a tone module to a basic keyboard-sequencer system. If the sequencer has a MIDI THRU jack, it should be used instead of OUT; if MIDI OUT is used, the ECHO ON (or THRU ON) setting should be made.

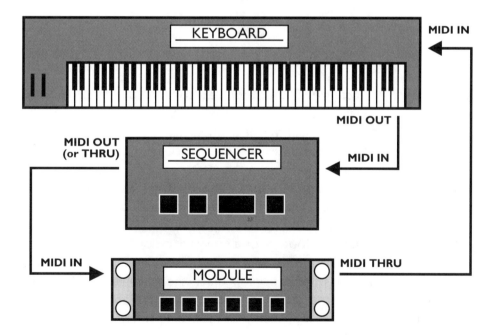

Figure B Another way to add a tone module to a sequencer.

range on the keyboard, program-change ability, and other settings that determine exactly how each sound patch will respond to incoming data (these settings are explored further in chapter 14).

Every tone generator has its own way of organizing its internal features, so it is difficult to give specific instructions here. Using your manual, you will ultimately create an ensemble of sound patches responding to different MIDI channels; this will be the "orchestra" you record with track by track, instrument by instrument. And the "members" of this orchestra will probably change with every piece you record.

Trying It Out

You're ready to create sequences using the expanded palette of sounds provided by the tone module.

As a test, first record a track using one of the keyboard sounds to which you've assigned a MIDI channel. Then add a second track with one of the tone module's sounds. You should hear the first track play back as you do this. Now play back the sequence; you should be listening to both tracks. Enjoy!

Producing a Soundtrack

Much of the most interesting MIDI music we hear today is soundtrack music. This is a broad category, ranging from film scores, which often use a mix of MIDI and acoustic instruments, to the music we hear underneath television commercials. Any music that exists to support some other piece of programming is called "underscoring." Producing such music in the MIDI domain has its own technical challenges. Because I've done quite a bit of underscoring for books on tape, I'll use that process to illustrate a typical MIDI underscoring job.

Because soundtrack music is composed and produced to accompany something else, whether it be video footage or a story narration, it helps to start with that other element. Typically, music is one of the last elements to be added to the final product. With a recorded book project, the story reading is recorded first. In my productions, the reader's performance is captured directly to computer hard disk by means of specialized recording software. The recording is digital, and storing it on computer makes it easy to execute necessary editing operations. These operations involve stringing the various "takes" together into a coherent whole, so in the end it sounds like an unbroken reading. When this is done, the performance can then be transferred to DAT (digital audio tape).

At this point, the composer's work begins. From the DAT, I make a cassette copy of the reading. This is my "work" copy. I use this tape in a four-track cassette deck. Because the reading, recorded in stereo, takes up two tracks, this leaves two tracks free. I only need one of these free tracks, which I'll use to record time code from the computer. This is the recorded tone that, when played back into the computer through a time code translator, controls the recording and playback functions of my sequencing software. This way, when I start and stop the cassette deck, the computer starts and stops along with it. This enables me to shuttle back and forth to various parts of the story, adding musical elements as I am actually hearing the narration. These musical parts are not recorded to the tape; they are saved to disk as MIDI files.

When this process is finished for the whole story, it's time to master the musical elements (called "cues") by recording them to DAT. I now have one DAT with the recorded story, and another with the musical cues that will eventually play underneath the story. Time to move into postproduction.

Postproduction is the process of assembling all of the produced elements into a finished product. First, the narration is transferred from its DAT to one track of multitrack tape. Then the music is recorded to two other tracks (because it's in stereo) of the same multitrack tape. This is easier said than done, because it must now be synchronized by hand and ear with the story. Time code is of no help here, because the music isn't coming from a computer, but a tape. It's important to go into the postproduction studio with a written cue sheet that describes the exact moment (usually a word of the story) where each music cue begins.

After this comes the recording of whatever sound effects will be included. The final step is mixing. Here, all the elements, which have been assembled and synchronized onto one multitrack tape, are balanced in relation to each other, so the music supports the story without interfering with it. The final mix is recorded onto some permanent stereo-tape format, often DAT, from which it can be duplicated and packaged.

There are almost infinite variations to this process, depending on the project. Video underscoring requires different equipment and procedures. But all production and postproduction share one rule, a rule that every producer lives by and that governs the process from beginning to end: do whatever works.

IV

MIDI
TOPICS

14

Understanding Your Keyboard

Up to a certain point, digital keyboards are easy to use. Once out of the box, plugged in, and turned on, most of them will deliver a sound when played. Changing from one sound to another is also usually simple. This may be enough for musicians who are using the keyboard as a surrogate piano, but it isn't enough for those players who are interested in developing a system, recording, or creating new sounds. Exploring these deeper levels of keyboard capability has rewards, but the learning curve is steeper and requires a different approach than the usual way we have been accustomed to learn about acoustic instruments, and also requires learning the new digital-music vocabulary.

Many people discover that the owner's manual for their new keyboard is not too helpful in facing this learning curve. In MIDI's early days, this was often due to the language barrier between an English-speaking consumer and the Japanese equipment manufacturers. This is less of an issue today, but an owner's manual still can only teach you the specifics of one particular keyboard. Manufacturers usually assume that you have some general knowledge of MIDI and keyboards, and they cannot reasonably be expected to offer a general education on these topics. Many in fact do devote some pages to a quick, valiant attempt at a MIDI overview; nevertheless, for many people, enlightenment by owner's manual is a throw-your-hands-in-the-air experience.

Every keyboard has different features organized in different ways. Manufacturers may also use different terms to describe sounds, programs, and functions. But manufacturers of digital music devices, perhaps more than most branches of technology, understand the value of compatibility; it is that understanding, after all, that begat MIDI in the first place. It is not to their advantage to release a keyboard that is unique in operation and vocabulary, because it would be too difficult for most users to integrate it into their systems. Rather, manufacturers strive for uniqueness in sound while maintaining friendliness in the machine/user interface.

This chapter focuses on the general ways all keyboards work and covers some important variations. By the end of the chapter, your owner's manual will make more sense, and you'll be able to get more out of your keyboard.

It's not called that in my manual!

I know, I know. Manufacturers seem to take a twisted pleasure in creating unique, esoteric vocabularies for their products. You may find any number of variations on the programming terms presented here. This is a test of your patience and ingenuity. You might find, for example, VCF (for Voltage Controlled Filter) instead of, simply, filter. If I were to detail every possible term you might encounter, this book would read like a laundry list.

How Keyboards Are Organized

Although it may seem strange at first, it is helpful to think of a keyboard as essentially a specialized music computer that can perform functions on several different levels. How these levels of operation relate to each other (and to you) is known as the keyboard's architecture. The levels of a keyboard's architecture include: creating, playing, and organizing sounds; accessing and controlling sounds in other MIDI instruments; and transferring and sometimes recording data. Although we hear the result of all this as sound and music, as far as the keyboard is concerned it's all just data. Almost everything that happens inside a keyboard is computation of numbers; only at the very end of those computations (though it all happens so quickly as to seem instantaneous) is the data translated from digital to analog information that, when amplified, can be understood by our ears.

Waveforms

In looking at how the keyboard (and you, the user) can build the sounds we hear, our starting point will be the smallest, most basic building block that a keyboard has to work with.

If the anatomy of sound can be said to have a shape, that shape is a wave. It is in undulating waves that sound travels through the air and stimulates our aural sense, and it is in the form of a wave that sound is drawn in a graphic image. The shape of a sound wave defines the quality of the sound. A simple, uncomplicated, repetitive sound wave represents a pure, unchanging sound; a complex wave of shifting form yields a more complex, changing sound. Acoustic musical instruments tend to generate complex sound waves. If we were to analyze the sound of a single note played on the piano, we would see that there are different "portions" of the sound, and that the wave shape changes drastically over the time that the note is audible. The sound starts when the piano hammer hits the string, and this brief element of sound is primarily percussive; then the sound wave swells as the string's vibration begins and is amplified by the soundboard; there is a short period of sustain in which the note may not be audibly fading; finally there is a longer period of decay during which the sound fades away. Of course these elements combine in our ears to form a single sonic entity: a note. But if any of the elements were removed, the note would begin to sound unnatural.

Sound waves are the smallest building blocks in a keyboard's architecture. Every keyboard comes stocked with a selection of preset waveforms that it processes and combines to make the most natural-sounding tones possible. This library may consist of two basic types of waveform: synthetic and sampled. Synthetic waveforms are simple, repetitive waves such as sine, square, and saw waves. In their pure, unprocessed form they produce an unchanging sound that starts abruptly and sustains at the same level until the note is released. A sampled waveform is a digital recording that has been produced by acoustic or natural means. It could be a note of a violin, or a dog's bark, or the wind. This sample of sound is stored in the keyboard's memory chips along with the synthetic waveforms.

Samples take up more room on the keyboard's internal chips than do synthetic waves because of their complexity. Because an artificial waveform is so simple, it can be represented in the keyboard's memory as a single wave cycle that simply repeats over and over when played. The single cycle, by itself, might last only a thousandth of a second. A good representation of a sampled acoustic sound, though, will probably last several seconds; because the sound changes so much during that time, it cannot simply be cycled. A sampled wave, then, requires thousands of times more data than a synthesized one, and these samples take up most of a keyboard's waveform memory.

A keyboard's library of sampled sound waves is permanently installed in its ROM chips and cannot be erased. The waves are a permanent part of the instrument's software, and they are a large part of what you are paying for when you buy a keyboard. Though you will almost never hear a sample in its "raw," unprocessed form, the overall sound of the keyboard, pleasing or not, is based on the quality of its waveforms. Much depends on the care with which the manufacturer created this software; in other words, how well the samples were recorded, the quality of the original source of the samples, how naturally the samples are looped, and how many samples were taken to represent the entire keyboard range.

The waveform library is likely to contain samples of many common acoustic instruments and instrument groups. A selection of synthesized waveforms is usually present as well. You might wonder why, considering that these waveforms are less natural sounding than samples. For one thing, it is not the only goal of a keyboard, or some keyboard players, to simply imitate the sounds of other instruments. Synthetic waves can be used to construct new, original sounds; indeed, this was all that synthesizers could do before sampling was invented. An "unnatural" sound can still be a beautiful and useful one, and many MIDI composers consider sound creation to be part of the composition process. Also, the sound of a raw sample is often enlivened through combination with a synthesized sound. A flute sample, for example, may be deepened and actually made to sound more realistic when combined with a sine wave.

Sound Programs

When we speak of a raw waveform, we are referring to the sound wave as it was recorded (sampled) or synthesized, without any alterations. When you first turn on a keyboard and play it, you almost never hear a raw waveform. The preset instrument settings are processed versions of the original sound waves. Raw, untreated sound waves usually do not sound very good, and are not very useful musically.

Most professional model keyboards include a group of settings for altering raw waveforms. These settings control tone-generating modifiers that can change the way a sound begins, sustains, and ends; its tone quality; and which waveforms contribute to the sound. While it is not possible to take a flute sample and make it sound like a violin, it is possible to make its tone brighter or more muted, or create a natural and graceful fade to the end of its notes. These programming tools usually are not found in home keyboards, which partly explains the difference in sound quality between the home and pro models.

The result of this processing is the sound program, alternatively called a sound, a program, or a patch. The presets you hear when you first turn on a keyboard are patches—waveforms that have been treated by the keyboard's programming functions. Using these functions is called programming or editing a sound, and the settings for accomplishing this are found in a section of the keyboard's architecture usually called "program edit" or something similar. Remember that we are talking about the internal architecture of the keyboard, not a section of front-panel buttons (though at least one popular model reverses this tendency by putting all its programming controls right on the front panel with buttons and data sliders). This internal section, and others, are *accessed* with the front-panel buttons, and the user navigates through the section with the help of the LCD screen that displays, in more or less graphic form, the available settings.

The program edit section can be very large, with dozens or even hundreds of possible settings. The settings are called "parameters," and are organized into subsections sometimes called "pages." The parameters are occasionally of the on/off or yes/no variety, but most of them offer a range of possible values, such as 00–99. Taken as a whole, the keyboard's ability to process waveforms is known as its "programming hierarchy" or "synthesis engine." Even if programming new sounds is not your main interest, it is useful to know the basic programming functions of your keyboard and the meanings of programming terms. Many people habitually make small changes in the preset patches, tailoring the details of their sound; this is called "tweaking."

Do I have to program?

There are two kinds of people in this world: those who enjoy creating new sounds, and those who would rather leap off a tall building into a vat of pudding (chocolate).

You don't need to program your synth to enjoy it or use it positively. You may be completely satisfied with the factory sounds, and you can always acquire new patches from other programmers.

However, there is a middle ground. Sometimes a patch just needs a slight adjustment of its parameters to make it more useful. Perhaps the release rate on the envelope of a violin sound needs to be lengthened a bit, so the sound doesn't cut off as quickly when you release the key. Or maybe the filter setting needs to be increased on an electric piano patch, so the sound will be less biting. Making these adjustments is called "tweaking." It can be good to know the basics of your synth's programming parameters, so you can tweak as needed.

But only if you want to. You can get out of the pudding now.

You'll find that many pages of the program edit section are devoted to "envelope" settings. A sound's envelope, quite simply, is what happens to it over time. It includes every change we hear in a sound from its very beginning until it fades away. Earlier, when we analyzed a piano note and found that it could be divided into beginning, sustain, and decay portions, we were really describing its envelope. All envelopes (and therefore all sounds) are viewed in terms of attack (the very beginning of the sound), sustain, and decay. These are only the most basic reference points of an envelope; most keyboards include additional points for controlling the envelope shape, including a release setting, which determines how the sound fades after the key is released. This may sound a bit confusing; often the best way to get comfortable with envelopes is to experiment with the settings and listen to what happens to the sound.

Envelope settings are either time or level settings that determine, respectively, how long it will take for the sound to get to the next portion of the envelope, and what its level (volume) will be when it gets there. Here's an example. The attack is the first portion of an envelope, and you will be offered two attack settings: time and level, each with possible values of 00–99. If you set the level first, and assign it a value of 99, then you will have the loudest possible attack. The only question is how long it will take for the beginning of the note to reach that level. If you set the time at 00, the attack will be instantaneous, and when you press a key you'll get a sudden, loud tone. If you set the time value at 35, the sound will take a bit of time to swell up to its full attack level. (These time values usually do not represent seconds or any other "real-time" increment.) The same time/level control is possible for each stage of the envelope; the number of stages depends on the keyboard. (In the real acoustic world, sound envelopes are completely smooth in their gradations of change; assigning them stages is necessary as a programming tool.) The owner's manual for your keyboard probably uses pictures of envelope shapes to explain the stages that can be implemented in your particular instrument (see Figure A).

Envelope control is useful for improving and tailoring a waveform, but it is essential when it comes to raw synthetic tones. Unprocessed artificial waves are unnaturally static and unchanging, but by manipulating their envelopes they can be turned into more graceful and usable sound programs. Even samples often require some envelope shaping, though this is truer for longer, sustaining samples such as those of bowed strings and wind instruments. Drum and percussion samples, by contrast, usually do not last long enough to allow for any shaping, and if they are recorded (sampled) well in the first place, can be used effectively in their raw form.

We're not finished with envelopes yet. There are three different aspects of sound that can be shaped, so that every sound actually has three multistage envelopes: the volume (loudness) of a sound, its tone quality (brightness, dullness), and finally its pitch can vary over time. Most keyboards use standard terms to refer to these different envelopes. The amplitude envelope controls volume changes; the filter envelope regulates the tone quality; and the pitch envelope makes changes in pitch.

You may be able to control the envelope even further according to how you actually play the sound. There are two common ways to do this found on many keyboards. One regulates the setting of an envelope stage according to the velocity (the force) with which a key is struck. A useful example would be to regulate the attack-time setting—the amount of time the sound takes to reach its full attack volume—so that a quick start is produced when you play loud, and a slower attack

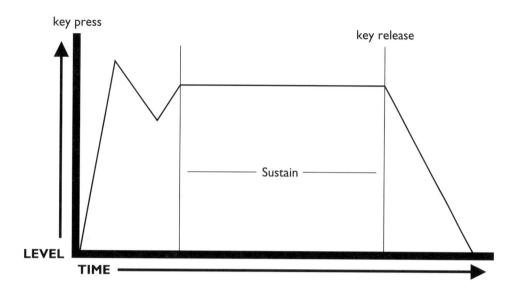

Figure A   A five-segment envelope. Envelope stages go by various names depending on the synthesizer.

is generated with softer playing. This is rather detailed programming, but very well worth experimenting with if you are interested in obtaining the most expressive, natural-sounding patches possible. Some keyboards offer this type of control over many stages of all the envelopes. The second type of control will affect the envelope according to where on the keyboard you're playing. This is called "keyboard tracking"; one typical example would be setting the filter envelope so that the sound becomes brighter as you move up the keyboard range. When combined with some kind of velocity-sensitive control, the envelopes can work together to make a once-raw waveform respond to keystrokes in a much more flexible and realistic fashion.

Licking the envelope

The envelope generators in synthesizers can be as aggravating as a bad pun. Here are a few starting points for addressing an amplitude envelope, the more common type.

- Increasing the attack time slows the beginning of the sound. If you increase it enough, the sound will "fade in" very slowly.
- Increasing the attack level makes the beginning of the sound louder.

- Decreasing the decay level makes the sound fade more drastically as the key is being held down. If the decay level is kept as high as the attack level, there will be no fade at all, as long as the key is held.

- Increasing the decay time causes the sound to fade more slowly while the key is held down.

- Increasing the release time makes the sound fade more slowly after the key has been released.

These descriptions are for amplitude envelopes, which affect the volume of a note. Filter envelopes affect the tonal quality (higher level settings cause a brighter tone), and pitch envelopes change the pitch (higher level settings cause a higher pitch). Although the three envelope types work together and affect each other, the settings can usually be adjusted individually, so each envelope has a different shape.

Let's take a quick look at some of the other parameters that may be found in a keyboard's program edit section. Filters have an important effect on a patch's sound quality. In addition to the filter envelope, most keyboards include one or more independent filters, which give you an overriding control over a sound's tone quality, regardless of what the envelope does to the sound over time. These filters are similar to simple equalizers or tone controls on your home stereo amplifier. They work by including, excluding, or emphasizing certain sound frequencies. (In acoustics, frequency refers to the speed with which a sound wave repeats its form. A slowly repeating wave is lower in pitch than faster waves. This has nothing to do with how quickly sound waves move through the air; they all move at the same speed.) Filters that emphasize upper frequencies and exclude lower ones will create a more treble sound, while reversing the filtering emphasizes the bass.

In keyboards, there are three basic kinds of filters, though any particular keyboard may not have all three. High-pass filters will allow the sounding of all frequencies above a selected frequency. Low-pass filters allow only lower frequencies to pass through. Resonance filters emphasize a narrow band of frequencies immediately surrounding a selected frequency. As with the time settings in the envelopes, filter settings do not relate to any real-world values. A little experimenting can take you a long way toward getting the hang of the filters.

The low frequency oscillator (LFO) is a programming parameter that creates a vibrato effect, or a light wavering of the tone's pitch. This is used to recreate acoustic instrument sounds that naturally produce vibrato, such as wind instruments, strings, and guitar. On most keyboards, you can regulate the speed and depth of the vibrato, as well as defining the delay, which determines how long after the key is pressed the effect will begin. The LFO is sometimes called a pitch modulator.

Many keyboards include digital signal processing (DSP) within their program edit parameters, and this can make a dramatic difference in sound quality. DSP is another term for digital effects, such as reverberation (reverb). As a DSP effect, reverb is a digital imitation of a natural phenomenon, namely the bouncing and echoing of sound waves off reflective surfaces. Most bathrooms are quite reverberative, because of their small size and hard surfaces. Concert halls are also, but in a different-sounding way. You can hear the largeness of a concert hall. Digital reverb mimics the reflective properties of different enclosed spaces and allows you to choose the sonic environment in which your patch will be played. Other digital effects are usually included, and sometimes two or more effects can be combined in a single patch.

One final function common to every keyboard that allows even minimal programming is the ability to name and store the newly created patch. Keyboard sounds are stored in banks, each bank containing a certain number of slots into which patches can be placed as if in cubbyholes in a desk. The instrument comes supplied with a preset bank of factory patches that usually cannot be erased (they are part of the keyboard's ROM, which can be accessed but not changed or deleted). If it seems like they can be erased, there is probably an "initialize" function that restores them when it is activated. Besides the preset bank, there will be a user's bank for storing programmed variations of the presets and new sound creations. (This is sometimes called the "internal" bank; an odd term because all banks are internal.) This bank is in the RAM section, which means the data can be accessed, changed, erased, and overwritten. RAM is usually backed up by a battery; this is called nonvolatile memory, and it means your saved patches will be retained even when the keyboard's power is turned off.

This description of a typical program edit section may seem inadequate if your keyboard has a particularly powerful synthesis engine with an extensive programming hierarchy. Beyond the basics covered here, there is great variation among keyboards.

Multiprogram Settings

Just as sound waves can be combined to form sound programs, so those programs can be combined to make performance setups.

The function of these setups depends on whether the keyboard is being used for live playing or for recording. Several patches can be combined onto one MIDI channel, so that they are all sounded when the keyboard is played. This can create a sound larger and more complex than a single patch could produce. When setting up the keyboard for recording with a sequencer, though, each patch is assigned its own MIDI channel so that they can be recorded independently (this important function will be discussed in more detail later). The preset multi setups included in most keyboards are usually programmed for live performance, so that the multitimbral power of the instrument can be sampled just by playing it.

This section of a keyboard's architecture is usually called either "multi," "combination," or "performance." Like the program edit section, it is organized in pages that group together common parameters. The number of patches that can be combined in this section is typically six, eight, or sixteen, and this number determines how many parts the keyboard's multitimbral function can support. This number may be different depending on whether you are setting up the patches for multichannel response or not. Some keyboards are designed to be primarily performance tools, and some are geared more for the studio. A keyboard may allow a different patch to be assigned to each of the sixteen MIDI channels, yet may not allow more than one patch to be assigned to any single channel—thereby facilitating recording, but discouraging patch-layering for performance.

In the first page of the multi section, you'll be able to select desired patches from the preset or user banks. There will be a separate page for assigning MIDI channels to the patches; this is where you'll find out if you can assign them all to one channel, give each its own channel, or both. Another page will allow you to determine the keyboard range for each patch in your combination. You might want one combination to be played only in the left-hand range, and another perhaps only in the top few keys. These ranges are defined by setting a low note and a high note, according to octave number and key letter.

Other pages may allow you to transpose each patch in increments of half-steps, set a volume level for each patch, and indicate how each patch will respond to velocity levels, aftertouch, damper-pedal signals, and program changes.

As with the sound programs, once a multi setup is created, it can be named and stored in a user bank. The preset multi bank, though—unlike the preset program bank—is often not placed in the permanent ROM portion of the keyboard's memory. In this case, take care to save the factory bank to a disk or a RAM card if its settings would be useful in the future.

Global Settings

The final, highest level of a keyboard's organization contains settings that affect the entire instrument. The master tuning function is found here. It is not a transpose feature, but a finer pitch regulator that can pull all the patches up or down by fractions of a semitone. There may also be a master transposer in the global section, for shifting from key to key. Setting the global MIDI channel determines what channel the keyboard will transmit and respond to when it's in the program mode. There may be MIDI filtering options in the global section, enabling you to decide which parts of the MIDI controller data will be accepted. You might, for example, want to filter out program changes so that the keyboard does not switch patches in response to another controller's program changes (see Figure B).

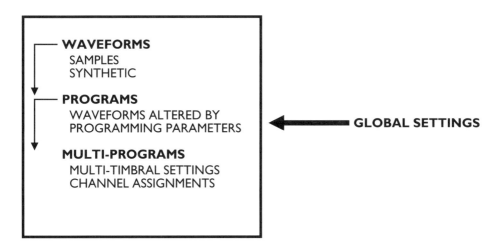

Figure B Most keyboards are organized in the same basic way.

Learning to Program

One of the greatest uses for computers lies in helping program synthesizers. Sound creation is greatly assisted by a computer, which can simultaneously display many programming parameters. But, as I can attest from personal experience, it's not necessary. I began making new sounds on my first synth, before my first computer was a gleam in my eye. There may be advantages to learning from the ground up, without the processing power of a computer. Whether a computer is available or not, here are a few ideas to keep in mind:

- Treat programming as a sonic adventure.
- Have fun.
- Experiment.

When I first began my programming experiments, I soon learned that the envelopes are the trickiest parameters to manage and to understand. They are also the most rewarding parameters to play with, because they affect the sound so dramatically. The best way to learn about the envelopes of your particular instrument is to fiddle with them endlessly. Again, this is an entirely different experience with a computer than without one; almost all computer sound-editing programs contain graphic representations of the envelope shapes, which makes it much easier to "see" the sound as you shape it. But if you don't have a computer, being forced to visualize that shape on your own may, in the long run, teach you more about how envelopes work.

There are two basic aspects to mastering envelopes. One is learning how the individual envelopes work, and the other is discovering how all the envelopes work together. Your instrument may have a separate envelope generator for each oscillator, and you may be able to combine multiple oscillators in a patch. Furthermore, the synth may have envelopes for volume, filter (tone), and pitch. All these envelopes play themselves out simultaneously, interacting with each other, every time you press a key.

One of the most basic changes you can make when creating a new sound is to substitute waveforms. After you've made your sound and saved it, simply try assigning different waveforms and samples to the oscillator(s), and see how they work with the other settings you've made. The results can be surprising, and lead to ideas for other sounds.

Programming can be an evolutionary process. You may create one sound and save it; then substitute different waveforms, and save that; keeping those waveforms you'll change the filter settings to brighten or darken the sound and save that. This will lead you to try other samples with those settings, which will cause you to tweak the envelope settings a bit before saving . . . you get the idea.

After much experimenting along these lines, a wondrous thing may happen: you actually begin to get a sense of how it all works, so that when you get an idea for a sound you want, you know how to get it! This is perhaps the highest form of sound programming. But even if it never happens, remember that the real fun lies in experimenting. Enjoy your new sounds!

15

Third-Party
Products

The electronic manufacturing industry is like a road riddled with potholes. There are always gaps that can make for a bumpy ride for the customer of each manufacturer's products. To fill these gaps, secondary products have been developed that may not be entirely necessary to our musical well-being, but are useful in ways unforeseen by the original manufacturer. In the MIDI marketplace, many of these secondary products cover potholes and make our ride smoother. Some are necessary; some make life in the MIDI studio easier; others are merely fun. Some are "hard" products, others are services or software.

The companies that conceive of, manufacture, and distribute these support products are called third-party companies, because they represent a third part of the customer-manufacturer equation. Many of these enterprises are small; some are no more than a single person who fills a particular "pothole," such as new sounds for a certain synthesizer. Because of this, much third-party business is transacted through the mail, though some of these products can be found in music stores. The full range of third-party products and services can be seen within the pages of technical music magazines.

Third-party Sounds

The moment a new keyboard is released, advertisements appear to offer new sounds for it. This is an indicator of the hunger for variety that is typical of the MIDI enthusiast, as well as a general dissatisfaction with factory presets. This is not universally true, however. Modern keyboards sound much better off the shelf than they used to, and many people remain happy with the original sound selection for years. Still, almost every modern keyboard includes some means for adding new sounds, commonly either a built-in disk drive or a RAM card slot. The keyboard manufacturer itself will usually develop a sound library for its instruments, but often not as fast as the third-party developers, whose living is based on programming sounds for various instruments. The business is extremely competitive, and the happy result for MIDI consumers is the availability of large numbers of sound programs, often sold for a song (so to speak). Specialized banks of patches are sold for all kinds of musical genres and needs—from dance music, to film scoring, to new-age sonic textures.

These sounds are often packaged on floppy disks. If the keyboard lacks a disk drive, sounds may still be purchased on disk and loaded into the instrument through a computer. Disks may be formatted for a specific editor/librarian software program or be written in a more generic format that automatically extracts the sounds and loads them into the instrument.

Some people use rack-mounted MIDI disk drives (these are described in chapter 9) for storing, accessing, and loading sounds. Performers appreciate these units because they can be racked into a traveling case, thereby combining portability with the convenience of floppy-disk storage.

Another method is to buy the sounds on RAM card. This is the most portable method of carrying sounds. Most keyboards (if they have RAM card slots) can read sounds directly off the card without loading them into the instrument's RAM, thus doubling the number of patches available at any one time—a very important consideration in a performing situation. With RAM cards, it might not be necessary to take any disk drives to the gig.

By taking advantage of third-party sound development, it is possible to build a large library of sounds for your keyboard. Some of the more popular instruments have thousands of sounds available for them. This is a relatively inexpensive way to rejuvenate an instrument whose sounds have grown stale, and to expand its sonic palette.

Third-party Samples

Buying third-party sound programs is convenient in that all the necessary processing has been done to make them playable and effective patches. They may consist of samples, but they are not "raw" samples. They have been looped, their envelopes have been tailored; they might even have reverb added. They are ready to be played without any more work on your part.

Raw instrument samples are also available as third-party products, for those who want to expand their keyboards or sound modules on a deeper level. They differ from sound programs in a couple of ways. They are meant to be the building blocks of your original sound programs, using the voice-creation features of the keyboard. Their memory requirements also differ from sound programs that make use of the keyboard's factory samples. New samples take up much more memory.

Third-party samples for specific keyboards and tone modules usually come on ROM cards, not RAM cards as the sound programs do. This is because they are inherently more valuable than sound programs; samples are the building blocks of patches. They are a more basic part of the voice architecture, so it's important to store them in a way that they cannot be accidentally erased. Read-only memory (ROM) accomplishes this. In fact, the factory samples in a keyboard are also stored in internal ROM, whereas the patches are in RAM.

Samples require so much memory that they usually cannot be loaded into the keyboard; they are simply "read" right off the ROM card. In this way, the card effectively expands the internal memory of the keyboard, just as RAM cards sometimes do.

Third-party sound products for a sample-playback keyboard sometimes include a double offering of RAM and ROM cards. This way the customer is buying both new samples (on ROM) and new programs that use these samples (on RAM).

Third-party companies also supply support for samplers. Given these instruments' limitless and self-contained ability to acquire new sounds, you might think third-party support would be unnecessary. But sampling well is actually quite difficult, and the best results require good microphones, a quiet space, someone to play the instrument being sampled, and sometimes a good tape deck. It's important to sample many notes throughout the instrument's range, and they all must be consistently toned. In short, acquiring a professional-quality sample is a task best delegated to a professional sampling studio. This is not to say that home sampling cannot be effective—and quite a bit of fun. But for many the most efficient way to build a sample library is to buy it, relying on personal sampling only for specialized needs.

Third-party samples can be found in two broad categories: instrument specific and generic. Instrument-specific samples are those created for a specific sampler. They are formatted to be loaded directly into the sampler's internal memory, not recorded through the audio sampling input. These sample libraries, unlike collections of sound programs, are often created by the manufacturers of the samplers, because they are better equipped to undertake such a large recording project—recording dozens of acoustic instruments, note by note, under ideal conditions and processing the results so that they will sound good when they are loaded into their own sampler. They also realize, more fully than anybody, that a sampler's usefulness (and marketability) depends on the available library of sounds, because samplers (unlike synthesizers) are not equipped with any onboard factory programs. They don't make a sound until a sample is loaded in. Still, there are third-party companies that develop instrument-specific sample libraries. These are often small operations consisting of one person who uses a particular sampler, has become proficient at sampling for personal use, and has decided to turn the resulting library into income by offering it for sale.

Third-party firms have entered the picture in a larger way by developing generic sample libraries. These are collections of instrument samples recorded on a CD, tape, or CD-ROM that can be sampled by any sampler and are only available from third-party developers. They represent a more cost-effective way of building a library than buying instrument-specific sample disks, as a single sample CD may contain hundreds of samples. An instrument-specific disk might have only a dozen, or fewer, depending on the instrument and the integrity of the developer

Generic libraries require more work. The selections must be fed into the sampler through the audio input—in other words, the samples must be resampled—and then looped and otherwise processed before they can be used to good effect. Generic samples are raw. They are simple tones recorded as plainly as possible. Usually every tone of the instrument's range is represented in the recording, and you must resample them one at a time until a complete multisample is created. Then the processing begins.

There is a whole universe of generic samples. An owner of a sampler can shop among entire CDs of woodwind samples, percussion instruments, different popular synthesizers, or orchestral string sections. Some of these collections are available on CD-ROM, to be used with high-end samplers that can receive digital transmissions directly, bypassing the audio input.

Third-party Sequence Files

So far we have discussed sequencers only in terms of what we can create with them by means of recording. In fact, they can be used to play back other recordings, just like a cassette recorder that can play commercial recordings. Are there commercially released sequences? There certainly are. Third-party innovation strikes again.

There are a few common uses for third-party sequence files:

- Singers can buy MIDI recreations of popular songs, for both practice and performance.

- You can play back all kinds of music, from classical to rock. Part of the fun of doing this is that you can change the tracks and assign different instruments to the various parts.

- Sequenced rhythm patterns can be acquired and used as a basis for original (well, partly original) MIDI compositions.

- Sequence files can be shared among MIDI enthusiasts by uploading and downloading them to and from online electronic networks.

As with samples, there are two types of sequence files: sequencer specific and generic. Sequencer specific simply means that the sequence was created on—or has been adapted to—a specific hardware or software sequencer. These sequences can be loaded into that sequencer and played with a minimum of adaptation to the specific requirements of the sequencer. Sequencer specific files are available on computer disk for software sequencers, floppy disk for hardware sequencers that have disk drives, and cassette or generic MIDI disk format for hardware sequencers with no disk drive.

Generic sequence files are meant to be used with any sequencer, and come in a format known as the Standard MIDI File (SMF). This is a widely accepted format that nearly all software sequencers, and some hardware units, recognize and can load. There are two types of SMF: Type 0 contains a single track of multi-MIDI-channel data; Type 1 contains the unmerged multiple tracks of the original sequence. Type 0 is useful if you are loading a sequence that contains thirty original tracks, for example, into a different sequencer with fewer tracks. Once the single-track version of the sequence is loaded, the tracks can be separated to some degree. When track space is not a limitation, as between most software sequencers, Type 1 is more convenient, because the MIDI channels are already separated onto their own tracks.

Third-party Instrument Modification

No keyboard is perfect. No tone module includes every possible feature. No workstation is ideally designed for every user. After a new instrument has been on the marketplace for a while, has been reviewed by the magazines and used by musicians, its strengths and weaknesses become pretty well known. You may buy a workstation because of its superlative sampled sounds, only to find that its sequencer leaves a few things to be desired. A tone module with great polyphony and multitimbral specifications might have a limited selection of sounds.

Some third-party companies specialize in upgrading the specifications and enhancing the performance of MIDI instruments. One common upgrade is in the area of memory expansion. Adding memory chips to a keyboard or module enables greater storage of sound patches and samples. ROM and RAM upgrades are possible. Disk drive additions are also to be found, both floppy and hard drives. One popular upgrade involves MIDI retrofits of vintage, non-MIDI electronic synthesizers. These instruments are valued for their classic sound, but they are inconvenient to use in a MIDI environment because they don't "speak the language" and can't "talk" with sequencers and other keyboards. A retrofit makes them MIDI literate and equips them with MIDI jacks.

Third-party Information

You're holding a third-party information product; this book is a generalized source of information about the wide world of MIDI. Most third-party publications (or videos, or tapes) are more product-specific. Two factors contribute to the need for such information. For one, the owner's manuals that come with MIDI components are notoriously inadequate. This situation has improved, especially in the English documentation of Japanese-made products. The second factor is that experience using a particular component yields information that cannot practically be included in an owner's manual, which covers just basic operations. Many of these followup owner's manuals are written by individuals who have a deep understanding of an instrument's features and functions, and have evolved shortcuts to improve its performance.

These products can be in the form of books, tapes, videos, or combinations of all three. They are meant to augment the original owner's manual, and take you as deep as you care to go into the details of the instrument's operation and programming.

Exploring the world of third-party products is part of the fun of MIDI, and it also makes understanding and using the technology much easier. Although this book is mostly devoted to the larger, more basic components of a system, it is the smaller support products that fill in the gaps. They are like the glue that holds the entire MIDI world together.

16

Expanding

When and How to Add to Your Setup

One great benefit of MIDI is that it is automatically expandable. Components can be added to the setup without regard to the manufacturer. The result is that MIDI studios tend to grow, with different features and capabilities being added as your musical and studio skills develop and as your finances allow.

It's possible that expansion will never be a temptation. There are many musicians who will derive years of challenge and pleasure from a basic keyboard/sequencer setup or a workstation. But for others, half the fun of the MIDI hobby is looking ahead to what will come next.

This chapter contains common sense information on expansion alternatives. Once you've narrowed it down to the type of component you want to add, you can refer to section 5.

Identifying and Filling Needs

Even the very simplest systems have strengths and weaknesses. From the first basic keyboard/sequencer system, or single workstation, every setup will shine in some ways and fall short in others. The first step is identifying your needs, then determining which of several alternatives fills those needs best. We'll assume a basic keyboard/sequencer setup; the sequencer may be built into the keyboard or stand alone as a hardware or software unit.

Recording

There is a wide range of features and power among sequencers, from the rudimentary recording ability of some home keyboards, to the most sophisticated software packages. When it is time to upgrade, a sequencer's deficiency is likely to be felt in at least one of four areas:

- Number of tracks
- Editing power
- Graphic interface
- Sequence storage

It is easy to see how limiting it can be to have fewer tracks than the sixteen MIDI channels. Because each MIDI channel can be devoted to a different musical part, it is convenient to record each part on its own track. Sequencers with eight, six, or two tracks can be sufficient at the beginning, particularly if the sequencer supports track-merging functions. But as your sequencing skills develop, it becomes more desirable to keep parts isolated on their own tracks to facilitate later editing.

Lack of editing power is likely to be the next frustration, which might be felt in these areas:

- Music data can't be controlled precisely.
- Individual MIDI events can't be easily manipulated.
- Tracks can't be merged or separated freely.
- Cut-and-paste options are not flexible enough.

If you're frustrated with weak editing features, you'd probably also benefit from a better graphic interface. Hardware sequencers give only the barest visual feedback on your editing, and many home keyboards give none at all. Recording and editing musical data is a brand new experience when you can see the data and the tracks.

Finally, if you're working with a sequencer that has no disk drive, you may be longing for an easier, less expensive way to store compositions. RAM cards are expensive and have a relatively small memory capacity, and cassette storage is cumbersome, slow, and has no random access.

The one solution that addresses all these needs at the same time is to use sequencing software on a computer, which offers:

- Up to hundreds of tracks (and at least sixteen).
- Varying editing power, but usually much more than hardware recorders.
- The wide-open graphics of a computer monitor, which is far superior to any LCD.
- External storage on floppy disks and hard disks.

But a computer can be an expensive investment, even with prices plummeting as they have been over the last few years.

If you are using a home keyboard, the next logical (and cost-effective) step might be to get a stand-alone hardware sequencer that offers more tracks, more power, and at least some minimal graphic feedback. A midrange model would be appropriate, and investing a bit more would get you a unit with its own disk drive.

If you have a workstation and are dissatisfied with its sequencer, a separate hardware recorder might also be the ticket, but you'll probably have to look at higher-end models to improve on your current editing power, and to get a disk drive. It is at this point that many MIDI enthusiasts take the plunge and buy their first computers. It can be a much larger investment (though not necessarily), but computers offer a quantum leap in power, ease of use, and flexibility.

If you are using a hardware sequencer, your choices are to upgrade to a better stand-alone unit, or think about purchasing a computer.

Sounds

The desire for more, different, and better sounds is one of the most common reasons for studio upgrades. The need for sounds shows itself in a few ways:

- Need for more variety. If the same MIDI equipment is being used frequently, you can easily tire of the basic preset sound library included in the instruments. The constantly evolving sound design represented in new instruments is seductive.

- Need for greater polyphony. All MIDI instruments have a limit on how many notes they can sound at one time. Bumping one's head against this polyphony ceiling can be quite frustrating; it can result in notes being cut off or not sounding at all. In this case, the need is for more voices, not necessarily different sounds. It is mostly a recording problem.

- Need for more realism and higher-quality sounds. Some MIDI components simply sound better than others. This is a function of many variables, but in general, higher quality sounds are included in less-expensive instruments all the time. So, even if more voices are not needed, there is the alluring prospect of upgrading the quality of available voices. This could mean more realistic samples, a higher level of synthetic timbres, or better digital-processing features.

- Need for a certain type of sounds. Sometimes there is a musical requirement for a particular instrument or type of instrument, such as ethnic drums, orchestral strings, or a realistic piano sample. The sound design industry has attained a degree of specialization, and these needs can now often be filled specifically.

There are two basic solutions to address your sound expansion needs: (1) acquire a new instrument or (2) upgrade the sounds of your present instrument.

Of course, you might not have a choice:

- Does your current instrument accept new sounds? Many home keyboards do not.

- Do you need more polyphony? In most cases, this indicates that a new instrument must be added.

- Do you need better voice synthesis features? If so, you need a new synth.

At this point, many people would acquire a tone module. There is a broad range of these modules available, and some contain sequencers, which might eliminate two problems at once.

Upgrading the sounds in your current instrument can be accomplished in a few ways:

- RAM card. If the instrument has a RAM card slot, you can buy a card that contains new sound programs.

- Floppy disk. If your instrument has a disk drive, you are using a computer, or you have an external MIDI disk drive, you can acquire new sounds on disk. If you're using an external disk drive, you may still have a problem, because your instrument may not accept new sounds over MIDI.

- Upgrade board. This is a circuit board that is installed directly into your current instrument, expanding the internal sounds, and perhaps changing other features of the instrument's operating system at the same time. These are usually made by third-party companies for specific instruments.

- Sample CD. If your instrument is a sampler, this is a very cost-effective way of acquiring new sounds. The sounds have to be resampled from the CD into the sampler, so it is not as trouble free as buying new sounds already sampled on disk. But it is less expensive, because you're buying a large number of sounds in bulk.

You can shop for sounds in music stores to some degree; a better overview of what's available can be found in technical music magazine ads. The advantage to browsing in a store, of course, is that you might be able to hear the sounds before buying them.

Storage

The time may come when you have all the recording power and sounds you need, but don't have the necessary storage options. Let's say your studio has expanded to the point of including a digital piano, a sound expander, and a hardware sequencer without a disk drive. At this point you are capable of creating fairly complex (and of course deeply inspired) multitrack pieces, but you have no way of saving your work. Your inability to store sequences is frustrating your musical growth.

On the other hand, let's say you have a portable keyboard, and have expanded your setup with a tone module. The module has no disk drive, and may or may not contain a RAM card slot. Even if it does, RAM cards are an expensive means of storing sounds. Your inability to save the new sounds you have created (beyond the internal saving capacity of the module) means you have to laboriously recreate them each time you play.

Again, a computer is the most drastic solution and would solve all your needs at once. But aside from the expense of the hardware, software would be needed to store sounds and sequences. Also, in upgrading to a software sequencer (which is how the sequences would be saved), you would need to learn how to operate in a new sequencing environment, one that would likely render your current sequencer obsolete. So a computer is indeed a radical solution, but one with huge benefits as well.

A generic MIDI disk drive would also be a systemwide solution and would enable you to keep your current components. These devices (described in chapter 9) enable you to save sounds and sequences to disk.

Other Expansion Options

Sequencing, sounds, and storage are the three primary areas of MIDI upgrading, but there are many other opportunities to upgrade a system.

Keyboard Controllers

Dedicated keyboard controllers create no sounds of their own and are used strictly to access sounds in other tone generators and to record data into a sequencer. The emphasis is on features that offer flexible data control and a satisfying playing feel. A truer "piano" feel is achieved through a full eighty-eight-key weighted action. MIDI channel splits are usually possible, so that the keyboard can transmit more than one channel at a time. Sometimes these keyboards have multiple MIDI outputs, for controlling more than sixteen MIDI channels. Typically, the master keyboard controller is the only keyboard in the system, or at least the only one whose keys are used.

Alternate Controllers

Some sounds are not effectively controlled from a keyboard, particularly if the original acoustic instruments from which the sample was taken are played differently, for example, wind and string instruments. An expansion alternative, then, is to acquire an alternate controller to make these sounds more persuasive.

Breath controllers provide more realistic control over wind-based samples. There are also drum pads for triggering percussion samples, MIDI pedals for hands-off access to bass sounds, and fingerstrips that offer expressive continuous controller commands such as pitch bending and vibrato.

MIDI Switchers

MIDI switchers organize your data streams and enable you to save different MIDI routings as patches that can be recalled with the push of a button. This can save you from the need to constantly rewire your MIDI connections. (MIDI switchers are described more completely in chapter 9.)

Instrument-specific Sequencers

Instrument-specific sequencers are sometimes made by the instrument's manufacturer and sometimes by a third-party company. They upgrade the sequencing features of a specific model keyboard. They can be found for digital pianos and for at least one workstation whose sequencer is not its strongest feature. There is not a very large market for these, as the advantage they hold over generic sequencers is small.

MIDI Retrofits

If you have an older, pre-MIDI keyboard, you may wish that you could add its sounds to your sequences, or access them from a MIDI keyboard. Some third-party companies specialize in retrofitting non-MIDI keyboards with MIDI capability. MIDI jacks are added, and the keyboard is made MIDI-literate, so that it is able to send and receive MIDI data. This can sometimes be done with acoustic instruments as well.

MIDI-controlled Signal Processing

A signal processor adds digital effects such as reverb, chorusing, and delay to the audio signal path (that is, the actual sound, not to the MIDI data). Such processing is often part of a keyboard's internal circuitry, but there are also external modules dedicated to producing these effects. Some of these contain MIDI jacks in addition to their audio inputs and outputs, to provide MIDI control over their operation. Parameters such as length of reverb time, or the reverb setting itself, can be changed according to the MIDI controller information being received. For example, the reverb decay time can increase (giving a "larger" reverb sound) when notes are being played loudly (i.e., when MIDI records greater velocity values). Or sending a MIDI program change (for the purpose of changing a patch in a tone module) can change the setting to an entirely different reverb setting (one that works better with the new patch).

Internal Hardware Expansion

Some specialized products, almost always made by third-party developers, offer changes in an instrument's operating system, and are meant to be installed directly inside the instrument. These replacement chips might: make a keyboard multitimbral if it isn't originally, increase the internal memory, change the MIDI channel implementation in some advantageous way, or increase the number of audio outputs.

MIDI Remotes

MIDI remotes are not on/off "zappers" such as we have for television sets. The most useful of these devices are remote programmers for creating new sounds in a keyboard or tone module. Sound programming is usually very difficult from the front panels of these instruments, because there aren't nearly as many buttons as there are parameters to be changed, and because the LCD displays are usually too small to accurately represent what you're doing. Remote programmers are an alternative to a computer, giving you control over the envelopes, filters, and other parameters in a more friendly way.

The Evolution of a MIDI Studio

If you have read this book to this point, you know more about MIDI than I did when I started my studio. At that point, I had no idea where this emerging hobby would lead me. As it turns out, it changed my life dramatically in a number of ways. Here's how my studio grew.

I began this addiction—oops, I meant to say passion—with a portable digital piano and a single tone module, purchased together. At the time, I was playing piano jobs in restaurants and bars, and I thought the digital piano would be useful for getting work in places that had no piano. The tone module was eight-part multitimbral; the keyboard could be split into two parts. For a pianist, this opened up a new world of sounds and possibilities, and kept me content for awhile.

I soon realized that the real power of MIDI lies in recording, and I began to shop for a sequencer. I settled on an eight-track model with a 20,000 note capacity and editing features that were considered powerful at the time. My first steps in MIDI recording taught me all about MIDI channels and MIDI tracks. Soon after, when I bought my first drum machine, I realized I was irretrievably involved with this new technology.

Sampling intrigued me. It took some time to save the money, but I ended up purchasing the state-of-the-art sampler of that year, a twelve-bit model that came with a whole library of sample disks. I was impressed with its warm sound and powerful synthesis capabilities. Now I had two keyboards, because the sampler only came in a keyboard version. The digital piano had a better keyboard, with seventy-six weighted keys instead of sixty unweighted ones; however, it was not as flexible as a keyboard controller. So I wanted to use both, but this required switching MIDI cables around whenever I wanted to record data generated from a different keyboard. This proved most aggravating, and before long I obtained my first MIDI switcher, an eight-by-eight model that allowed me to consolidate all my MIDI connections in one place, and switch from one studio configuration to another by just pressing a button.

With this arrangement, I was able to produce music for my own enjoyment, and I even began to get some professional jobs. These jobs began to determine the evolution of the studio, because I acquired what I needed as the needs arose. A digital reverb effects box gave a more spacious sound to my mixes. And speaking of mixes, I was quickly outgrowing the small, four-channel mixer that had been in my house for years. My next purchases were a larger mixer and a four-track cassette deck. The deck had another six channels of mixing built right into it, so I was set for a while.

It's at this point in the life of many studios that a big decision has to be made: whether to add a computer. For me the answer was clearly affirmative, because I had grown tired of the sequencer's difficult interface and relatively limited editing power. I bought a computer and sequencing software on the used market from another musician. I had also begun programming the tone module, and with the correct software, the computer made that task much easier. I soon realized that adding a computer is the single most significant upgrade that can be made to a MIDI studio, and I wondered how I had ever lived without it.

I now began collecting more tone modules in an attempt to broaden the range of sounds and textures my studio could produce. When you consider that my current rack contains seven modules and a drum machine, and that each instrument has at least two audio outputs, it becomes obvious that I've had to upgrade my mixer yet again. This upgrade raised the number of channels to twenty-four. I also became limited by the four tracks of the cassette deck, and purchased an eight-track reel-to-reel machine.

The studio is rounded out by such essentials as a dedicated power amp, several signal processing modules, a few patch bays, a pair of studio monitors (a fancy way of saying "speakers"), and a DAT (Digital Audio Tape) deck.

17
General MIDI (GM)

Compatibility is the founding concept of MIDI. By enabling various components to share a single data language, it has become possible to assemble MIDI systems that are essentially megainstruments. Play a sequence through one of these systems, and each instrument will receive, understand, and respond to the data.

But the compatibility doesn't extend completely to different systems. Let's imagine two MIDI setups. They each have keyboards, but not the same keyboard. They have different tone modules and sequencers. We create a sequenced song on the first system, using a particular arrangement of sounds and settings. If we now take that sequence to the second system and play it through different components, the result will be very different.

Why does this happen? Let's return to the first system for a moment. In order to create the sequence, you made many settings for each keyboard and tone module. Patches were chosen and assigned to MIDI channels. Relative volumes of the parts were set. Each voice's settings were adjusted for transposition, their position in the stereo image, program changes, tuning, and their responsiveness to all kinds of other MIDI data. Onboard effects were selected and/or programmed. In other words, the instruments were optimized for the music that would be recorded.

Take that sequence to another studio where the equipment has not been customized with the same settings and, even if the identical instruments are being used, the result will be musical gibberish. Every MIDI instrument has its own internal arrangement of voices. Even though there is overlap in the types of patches found in most keyboards, the actual samples and sound programs differ considerably, and, even more important, the arrangement of instrument types is never the same from one model to another. There are also differences in the operating systems among various components, affecting the degree of polyphony, multitimbral features, and response to MIDI controllers. The upshot of all this is the response of one system configuration to another system's sequence file is unpredictable. Take a simple piano and bass composition recorded in one MIDI setup, play it in another, and the composition is liable to be transformed into a duet for organ and trombone.

Because of this, sharing sequence files among systems—which you might think would be an obvious and typical benefit of MIDI compatibility—is actually very hard to do. It can be done, but requires assigning the voices used in the sequence to the correct program numbers then assigning them to the correct channels then assigning the drums to the same keymap. Only then can you play back a sequence from the first system and begin to get comparable results.

This situation has contributed to the difficulty beginners experience using MIDI systems. Until recently, MIDI sound modules have been like strangers who speak the same language but have very different customs. They can communicate, but it takes adjustment for them to work together.

To address this problem, the International MIDI Association has published a standard set of MIDI features to be implemented in any instrument that uses the General MIDI (GM) name and logo. GM is not a communications language, like MIDI, and it's not something that can be purchased and added to a component. What is it then? GM is an agreement among MIDI manufacturers about certain instrument settings and minimum operating standards. Its purpose is to make interchanging data among GM instruments easier.

General MIDI Specifications

All GM instruments are equipped with the following minimum standards:

- Twenty-four voice polyphony.
- All voices are velocity-sensitive.
- Sixteen MIDI channels.
- Drum and percussion sounds respond to channel 10.
- Each channel is responsive to certain basic continuous controllers.
- Inclusion of the GM "sound set."

This last is perhaps the most important, consisting of 128 sound types assigned to program numbers 1 to 128. On channel 10, specific drum sounds are assigned to specified MIDI note numbers. It is this assignment of voice types that is at the heart of GM's user-friendliness. Playing a GM sequence (that is, one recorded using a GM instrument) through any GM module will result in the correct instruments sounding, because the sound set is numbered in the same way in every GM module.

Acoustic piano will always be found as program #1, for example, and acoustic bass is always #33. The drums will likewise sound right without recreating a keymap, because the keymap is standardized.

This is not to say that all GM modules are the same in quality or sound characteristics. The sound set is a mix of specific instruments (like piano, trumpet, marimba) and sound *types*. In both cases, the descriptions in the GM specification are generic, and by necessity are ambiguous enough to leave room for different interpretations. Even though program #57 is trumpet, for example, each module will have its own trumpet sample in that slot. The ambiguity is even more pronounced with less specific instruments like electric piano and church organ, neither of which has clearly defined sounds. Numbers 81 to 104 of the GM sound set are described with particular vagueness. They are numbered lists of "lead," "pad," and "FX" patches with identifying names such as "fifths," "warm," and "goblins." Needless to say, there could be some variety in the interpretation of these sounds.

Advantages and Disadvantages of General MIDI

General MIDI takes some of the intimidation out of MIDI by standardizing the internal settings of GM modules. It simplifies the operations of the instrument, and makes MIDI more social, so to speak. With it, MIDI enthusiasts can share sequence files much more easily. If different GM models are being used in two systems, the results will not be identical by any means, but they will be comparable. At the very least, the correct patch will be heard playing every part. From there, adjustments can be made to optimize the instrument settings, if desired.

The future of General MIDI is not certain, but it is easy to see the ways in which it might grow. Third-party developers of sequence files can use it to create load-and-play sequences on GM instruments that can be effortlessly used by GM consumers. GM files will probably proliferate within the online networks, from which computer owners can download them. Indeed, MIDI beginners with computers represent a primary market for GM products. Some of the GM modules have computer interfaces, which means that the module can act as a MIDI interface for the computer, negating the need to acquire that particular piece of hardware. We might imagine the recording studio of the future as containing a "General MIDI room," where clients can transfer their GM sequences without the time-consuming and expensive process of customizing the studio's MIDI system.

But there are disadvantages to all this convenience. General MIDI doesn't always work ideally. There is basic compatibility, but the variety within the GM sound set yields uneven results that can only be smoothed out by means of the tweaking and programming that General MIDI was designed to circumvent. It is not only a question of different sounds being produced by different system setups. The GM specification is vague about data-response requirements with respect to velocity data and continuous controllers. Without getting too technical, this simply means that a well-balanced mix from one module might sound distressingly out of balance when transferred to another.

The upshot? GM modules are not as powerful as traditional MIDI components, but give you valuable conveniences. It is a trade-off of flexibility for ease of use, standardization for customization. In this way, General MIDI instruments are like autoexposure, autofocus cameras. You may get a good picture every time, but you lose the additional control that more sophisticated equipment offers.

V
SHOPPING FOR MIDI EQUIPMENT

This section is a buyer's guide to MIDI equipment, but not in the brand-comparing style of *Consumer Reports*. The product landscape shifts too quickly for me to attempt such a guide as part of a book. For reviews and discussions of specific models, it is best to keep abreast of the music magazines that specialize in electronic instruments.

Our goal here is to itemize the features you should look for (or avoid), and the questions that should be asked, when shopping for a MIDI component. At this point, we are assuming that you have a certain basic understanding of what these components are. If you have skipped ahead directly to this chapter and are unsure of just how a sequencer is used, for example, then you might want to read the relevant chapters in section 2 before using this shopper's guide. Section 3 wouldn't hurt, either, in giving you a picture of the hands-on requirements and potential problems of integrating a component into a system. But if you just can't wait, the gaps can always be filled in later.

18

Professional Keyboards

Product Profile

A vast selection of keyboards is available on the market today. Although there are MIDI controllers modeled on other instrument designs, digital control of music is undeniably biased toward the player of traditional black and white piano keys. During the last decade an astounding variety of instruments has been designed and manufactured, each with its own set of strengths and weaknesses. This makes shopping for a keyboard, particularly a first keyboard, both potentially more bewildering and, if done carefully, more rewarding than shopping for other components.

This chapter is devoted to "pro" keyboards, as defined in the earlier sections of this book and in the glossary. It excludes consideration of home keyboards, digital pianos, and workstations, which will all be covered in other chapters. Remember that professional keyboards are not just for professionals, and that the distinctions between professional and home equipment are getting blurrier all the time. The important thing is to know your needs, and select from the entire marketplace the keyboard that best fulfills them.

We will be considering the features of synthesizers and sample-playback keyboards that do not have built-in speakers or onboard sequencers. Such keyboards are often colloquially referred to as "synths," without regard to the relative strengths of their synthesis capabilities. Typical synths have sixty-one key, unweighted actions, an onboard selection of factory sound programs with some ability to alter and create new ones, and some capacity to store sounds externally. There is much variety within each of these categories.

Costs for new synths range from about $800 to about $5,000. The marketplace is so large, and changes so rapidly, that it is especially difficult to give an accurate range of costs without being ridiculously broad. The most popular synths for professional and home use are usually priced in the $1,500 to $2,500 range. As you can imagine, there is also an extremely active used market for keyboards, and preowned synths are generally considered to be a relatively safe buy, because they are comparatively sturdy and simple, with few moving parts. It is much safer, for example, to buy a used keyboard than a used tape deck.

Contemporary digital keyboards have evolved into very complex machines, with sophisticated processing power and expressive ability. At the same time, they are fun musical instruments, and many are easy to learn right out of the box. A truly comprehensive shopping guide is impossible, and not the intent here. Following are basic questions to keep in mind—and to ask—as you go through the shopping process.

Summary of Shopping Questions

1. Do you like the way the keyboard sounds?
2. Does the keyboard have a friendly user-interface?
3. What type of action does the keyboard have?
4. Does the keyboard accept new sound samples?
5. What kind of external storage does the keyboard offer?
6. How many preset sound programs does the keyboard offer?
7. What is the polyphony of the instrument?
8. What are the keyboard's multitimbral features?
9. How powerful is the keyboard's voice architecture?
10. What are the keyboard-control features?
11. Is the keyboard equipped with onboard effects?

Do you like the way the keyboard sounds?

It is easy when shopping for a technological component to become absorbed in technical specifications, when your satisfaction in the product will depend largely on whether it is musically satisfying; whether, in other words, it sounds good to your ears. Digital keyboards are musical instruments, each model with its own character, just as violins made by different craftspeople speak with their own unique tones.

Listening to all the preset sound programs is the best way to evaluate the character of a keyboard. One instrument might sound lush and "fat," while another is more crystalline and transparent. One might contain a beautiful piano sample; another, great drum sounds. One might be geared to playing classical music or jazz, while another is a pop instrument. One might have a deep selection of realistic instrument samples but weak programming control, while another might be stocked with only basic waveforms but be equipped with powerful sound-creation features.

It's important to shop with some idea of your tastes and musical needs. What kind of music will you be playing and/or recording?

Does the keyboard have a friendly user-interface?

How easy will it be to learn to use your keyboard and how accessible are its functions? The most important items of a keyboard's user interface are the LCD screen, sliders, and front-panel buttons that connect you with the instrument's inner workings. The front-panel controls translate your commands to the instrument's software, and the screen enables you to navigate through that software.

There are rules of thumb here. Naturally, the larger the screen, the more information will be conveyed, usually in an easier-to-understand (graphic) format; this makes life simpler. When reading keyboard specifications, screen size is usually measured in character numbers, referring to the number of letters and/or numbers that can fit on the screen. Thirty-two character screens are on the small side. Larger LCDs often enable envelope shapes to be displayed graphically, rather than as a table of numbers, and this makes programing sounds much easier.

Generally, the fewer buttons there are, the more cryptic and difficult the keyboard will be to operate and learn. This is because, in order to access all the internal functions, many of the buttons will necessarily have more than one purpose. What effect the button will have might depend on what part of the keyboard's software you are working in, or it might depend on what other button is being held down at the same time. In recent years, in response to customer feedback about confusing interfaces, manufacturers have designed front panels with more buttons. These keyboards may have a different button dedicated to each important function. This makes for a busy and, at first, an intimidating appearance; some of these instruments are bristling with controls. But learning how to use these keyboards can be much easier than struggling with sleeker instruments with buttons that serve double or triple duty.

Data-entry sliders and wheels are useful. They show that some design attention has been paid to making it easy to move through the large lists of numbers that are often encountered in programming new sounds, and scrolling through large numbers of preset sounds.

When shopping, try to learn something simple about the keyboard in the store, and see how long it takes to get fluent with this interface skill. For example, simply moving from program to performance mode (the actual names vary from one keyboard to another), and then returning to the sound you started with, should be relatively easy. Try moving from one sound to another, then back again. Create a simple multitimbral setup. Find out how to change the MIDI transmit channel (especially if you'll be using the keyboard with a tone module), and notice how many button pushes it takes to do this. Once you get your hands on a few different keyboards and can compare their ease of use, you'll get a feel for whether an instrument is friendly or unfriendly.

What type of action does the keyboard have?

A keyboard's action refers to the actual keys and the parts that are set in motion when you press them. There are two primary considerations: the size of the keyboard, and whether it is weighted.

All keyboards, except for the very least expensive home models, have keys of the same width as those on a piano. They are known as "full-size" keys. This is not to be confused with a full-size keyboard, however. A piano keyboard contains eighty-eight keys, but most digital keyboards are shorter. The most common size is sixty-one keys, which spans five octaves. The lowest note of these keyboards is C1, two octaves below middle C. An intermediate size contains seventy-six keys, which is shorter than a piano by only about half an octave at each end. And some keyboards are equipped with the full eighty-eight keys.

Typically, popular synthesizers and sample-playback keyboards have unweighted actions. The keys offer virtually no resistance when they are depressed, and, because of this, feel quite different from a piano, with its heavier mechanical action. It is very unusual to find a weighted sixty-one key action; more common to find weighted keys in the seventy-six key format; and quite common for the full-size keyboards to be weighted.

Again, it's important to consider how you will use the keyboard and what you are accustomed to playing. Classical players who want a keyboard for practicing piano repertoire would probably do better looking for a digital piano, because most of them have longer, weighted keyboards. Likewise, a player who plans on using the keyboard in live situations might look for a larger, weighted model, because many people find them easier to play accurately. If the keyboard is going to be used primarily in a studio, the sixty-one-key arrangement could be sufficient.

As you might expect, larger and heavier keyboard actions are also more expensive. Of course, these instruments are also heavier and less portable. Many models do not offer you a choice, so if you're in love with the sound, you may have to settle for whichever keyboard format is offered.

Does the keyboard accept new sound samples?

Some keyboards are more expandable than others. And no matter how much you love a keyboard when you first buy it, every experienced MIDI user will tell you this: the time will come when you'll grow tired of the factory-supplied samples, and will wish for some way of breathing new life into your trusty old (or not-so-old) keyboard.

If you look along the top or back of many keyboards, you will see a slot into which a credit-card sized object can fit. This slot is for memory cards. A memory card may contain any kind of data: sound samples, sound programs, sequences, or system-exclusive setups. What you're looking for is the capacity to load new sound samples into the instrument from a ROM card. These cards can be plugged into the slots and stay there indefinitely while you access the samples on them. In this way, you are actually expanding the memory of the keyboard.

Memory cards may be produced by the instrument manufacturer, or they may be supplied by third-party companies. During your shopping process, you should determine what libraries of new samples are available and how much they cost. Some keyboards accept only RAM cards, and these contain a different type of data. Samples are never stored on RAM cards. These memory expanders contain new sound programs using the factory samples that originally came with the keyboard. They are also good for rejuvenating the sound of an instrument, though not to the same degree as a card full of new samples. Some keyboards allow for both types of card, and the cards for these instruments are sometimes sold in pairs: a ROM card of new samples, and a RAM card of new programs using those samples.

What kind of external storage does the keyboard offer?

Here's a basic rule: no matter how much internal memory is included in a keyboard, it will not be enough. If you develop a taste for creating new sounds, or even if you simply need to make slight alterations to the presets, you will need to store these new programs. Most keyboards offer a certain number of program slots for new sound variations, but when they are used up sounds must be saved outside of the keyboard.

To accomplish this, the keyboard will either have a RAM card slot or a disk drive. Why don't all keyboards have disk drives? Partly for the customer's sake, and partly for the manufacturer's. Including a disk drive pushes up the cost of the instrument, even though it will save money later on. And the company that built the keyboard profits by selling RAM cards—both blank and loaded with new sound programs—as a separate product line.

How many preset sound programs does the keyboard offer?

This question is especially important if you are not as interested in sound programming and will be relying on the factory presets. In this case, more presets are obviously better than fewer. A typical range is between sixty-four and 200 factory sounds.

What is the polyphony of the instrument?

As we've discussed, polyphony refers to the number of notes that can be sounded simultaneously. The basic rule of thumb is that more is better, but there are several aspects to consider in determining how much polyphony is actually needed.

If the keyboard is going to be used primarily in a live performance situation, playing popular or rock styles, the ceiling can be pretty low. In these circumstances, the keyboard will be used to sound mostly simple chords and solo lead lines, and the sustain pedal is used minimally.

If the keyboard is going to be used as a surrogate piano, perhaps playing classical music with heavy use of the sustain pedal (causing notes to continue sounding after the keys are released, and thereby using more polyphony), a higher limit is required.

If the instrument is going to be used in a recording setup, where it will play back different simultaneously sounding parts in cooperation with a sequencer, polyphony is a serious consideration and should influence your purchase.

The days of six- and eight-voice polyphony are mostly behind us, and the minimum for contemporary keyboards seems to be sixteen voices. Some offer twenty, twenty-four, or thirty-two simultaneous notes (we're using "notes" and "voices" interchangeably here), and at this writing some companies are beginning to promote instruments with greater capabilities.

When you're reading instrument specifications and talking with salespeople, don't confuse notes with oscillators. An oscillator is what actually produces the sound we hear from a keyboard. Many instruments enable the doubling, tripling, or quadrupling of oscillators in the creation of a patch (sound). This makes for more interesting, "fatter" sounds. When more than one oscillator is contributing to a sound program, the polyphony of that sound is reduced. This is because every keyboard has only a certain number of oscillators. Naturally, when writing the specifications for their instruments, manufacturers will claim the highest polyphony they can, and so will often refer to the number of oscillators on board. Therefore, a sixteen-voice polyphonic keyboard usually (though not always) contains sixteen oscillators. But when you're playing a patch that uses two oscillators for every note, this keyboard can only produce eight-voice polyphony. This can be quite a shock when encountered unexpectedly. Exceeding the polyphonic limit causes notes that are sounding to be cut off prematurely.

What are the keyboard's multitimbral features?

Nearly all pro keyboards made these days are multitimbral; that is, they can play more than one part—each represented by a different instrument patch—at a time. Common multitimbral configurations are six, eight, or sixteen parts. Because the MIDI specification only allows for sixteen MIDI channels, and normally each musical part is recorded on its own channel, multitimbral capability beyond sixteen parts is not to be found.

There is also a question of how the voices are allocated in multitimbral operation, whether they are "dynamic" or "assigned," terms you'll often find in comparison charts in shopping guides. Dynamic allocation has become much more common, but assigned allocation is still occasionally found, especially if you're including used instruments in your shopping. Assigning voices is a more rigid system, and involves setting a limit to the number of voices (notes or oscillators) that can be used by any particular MIDI channel. When a part is received by the keyboard from a sequencer on a certain MIDI channel, it will only play it to the degree that the part doesn't exceed the assigned number of simultaneous notes. In other words, you are setting a polyphony level for each MIDI channel. Of course, you can only work within the overall polyphonic limit of the entire instrument.

Dynamic allocation, on the other hand, requires nothing from you to work, except of course that you must assign patches to MIDI channels. But you needn't worry about assigning polyphony, because the keyboard will simply "take" notes (oscillators) as needed to play each patch. You need be concerned only with exceeding the overall polyphonic limit of the instrument.

You might also want to check for this buzz phrase: "independent MIDI controller response." This refers to each channel's ability to respond independently to MIDI data such as pitch bends, aftertouch, and other miscellaneous controlling information. If the response is not independent, it is global, meaning that all your parts (each of which is assigned its own channel) will bend upward when you move the pitch-bend wheel on any one channel. All MIDI control data is recorded to a certain MIDI channel and played back on that channel; it is very helpful if the keyboard recognizes that and only responds on that channel. This has become a common feature, but not a universal one.

How powerful is the keyboard's voice architecture?

This question is relevant if you will be designing original sound programs. A keyboard's voice architecture is composed of all the settings that change the way a patch sounds. Some keyboards offer powerful sound-shaping features, and others are more rudimentary. The trade-off, as with all hardware and software, is that the more powerful the equipment, the harder it is to master. If a keyboard offers many sophisticated synthesis controls, it will probably be harder to learn how to use those controls, which might discourage a new user from experimenting with sound creation at all. So a balance should be sought between intimidating complexity and frustrating simplicity.

Look for filters. Changing filter settings is one of the easiest and most dramatic ways to change a sound, and often interesting and useful new sound programs can be created just by playing with the filters. There are different kinds, but all filters work by suppressing certain frequency ranges of the sound.

Some kind of envelope control should be present. Envelopes determine what happens to the sound over time, and are divided into programmable stages. The more stages there are, the more control you have, but again, the trick is to understand them. It is helpful to have different envelopes for the sound's pitch, tone (filter envelope), and volume (amplitude envelope).

It is particularly difficult to learn about an instrument's voice architecture before buying it. If you want a keyboard with strong programming features, you should read technical reviews before beginning your shopping process. The technical music magazines offer back issues for sale if you need to see a previously published review, and most will help you find the issue you need. Tracking down these reviews is time well spent.

What are the keyboard-control features?

Most of our questions have been concerned with a keyboard's internal software. It's also important to consider the keyboard simply as a MIDI controller, keeping in mind that it may be used as the master controller for a larger MIDI setup.

The keyboard should be touch sensitive, and most of them are. This simply means that when you hit a key hard you get a loud sound, and when you press gently you get a softer sound. Aftertouch is less common, but adds to the expressive control you have over the sounds. Aftertouch data is generated by pressing down on a key after you've sounded the note. The resulting controller data can influence different aspects of the sound, such as adding vibrato to the note or making it louder. Channel aftertouch adds the effect globally to every note currently being sounded, while polyphonic aftertouch enables you to apply the control data to individual notes, and is both more expressive and more unusual.

Many keyboards have one, two, or three wheels on the far left side of the front panel, next to the keys. These are expression wheels that affect the sound of a played note. The most common is a pitch-bend wheel, which bends the note up or down, depending on which way it is turned. The amount of the bend is usually programmable on a patch-by-patch basis, in increments of a half-step. Other wheels can add vibrato or tremolo, or be programmed to change some other aspect of the sound. As an alternative to the wheels, at least one major manufacturer uses a joystick design to obtain many of these effects with just one control.

One useful MIDI control feature is the ability to split the keyboard between more than one MIDI channel. We have spoken of keyboard splits in a different sense, because many instruments can deliver two different sounds from different ranges of their keyboards, both using the same MIDI channel. But it can also be useful to set the keyboard to transmit two different MIDI channels, separated by a split point, so that you can control different modules—or different patch/channel assignments within the same module—simultaneously from one keyboard. An example would be a setting that enabled you to play a bass patch on channel 2 (generated from module A) from the lower part of the keyboard, while also playing a piano sample (from module B) on channel 9 from the upper part of the keyboard.

Is the keyboard equipped with onboard effects?

Digital effects (otherwise known as digital signal processing, or DSP) are increasingly common features of modern keyboard design. This inclusion began when workstations first gained popularity, but now all kinds of keyboards, even inexpensive home models, often include at least digital reverb. Other common effects include:

- Chorusing: a stereo effect in which the right and left halves of the sound are tuned slightly apart from each other.
- Delay: a repeating, echoing effect.
- Aural exciters: an enhancement of the sound usually achieved by adding upper frequencies to it.

Reverb is the most basic digital effect, and the most necessary to give music a natural sounding spaciousness. It may seem strange that an artificial, digitally produced effect would make music sound more natural. But the samples that are the source of a keyboard's sounds are usually recorded "dry," without any of the natural echo that would be present if you were hearing the instrument in a room. Digital reverb attempts to restore that natural ambience, and it can make a huge improvement in the sound of a keyboard. This can be heard by playing the same patch first with the reverb on, then off.

If effects are included, most keyboards will have between one and four different processors. It is advantageous to have more than one, in order to layer one effect on top of another.

How to cope with a user-hostile keyboard

1. Cursing helps.
2. Write to your senator (just don't expect a response).
3. Sell it to an enemy (for more than you paid for it).
4. If you don't have any enemies, sell it to a friend who enjoys dealing with emotionally disturbed machines.
5. Perform magic rituals (such as burning your owner's manual) to exorcise the demon within the keyboard.
6. Try cursing again.

OK, maybe that's not the most helpful advice you've ever received; here are some real suggestions.

Call the technical product support phone number for the manufacturer. This number is sometimes printed in the owner's manual. If not, find a main number for the company and track down the technical-support division. If it's not a toll-free number, yell at them and tell them you'll call collect next time (and do it). When getting technical support, don't be rushed. Try to have the keyboard in front of you, so the tech-support representative can walk you through the steps.

If you have a computer, get a modem and join one of the online services. This way you can talk with many people who have probably solved the same (or similar) problems as the ones you're struggling with. Manufacturers also sometimes offer technical support online.

Look for third-party support for your keyboard. There might be books and videos that can help tame your snarling beast.

| 19 |

Hardware Sequencers

Product Profile

Stand-alone sequencers have become somewhat less prevalent as their software counterparts have become more so. But there is still a substantial demand for them among MIDI enthusiasts who either don't have a computer (and don't want to invest in one) or who need a more portable MIDI recorder.

Prices vary from about $200 to about $1,000, and that spread represents a tremendous range of features and power.

Strictly speaking, a sequencer is nothing more than a data recorder. But some models also contain a selection of sounds to record with; these can be considered tone module/sequencer hybrids. Most drum machines are equipped with rhythm-pattern sequencers, but they are not meant to record data from an external source.

Summary of Shopping Questions

1. How many tracks does the sequencer have?
2. How many notes will the sequencer hold?
3. Does the sequencer have a disk drive?
4. What editing features does the sequencer offer?
5. Is it a pattern sequencer?
6. What is the sequencer's range of tempos and time signatures?
7. What is the sequencer's timing resolution?
8. How does the sequencer's metronome work?
9. Is the sequencer easy to use (user-friendly)?

How many tracks does the sequencer have?

This is the first and most basic question about a sequencer's level of power, and the answer will tell you generally what to expect in the way of other features. A model with only two tracks, for instance, will probably not be equipped with the same editing power as a sixteen-track model.

You should consider how you plan to use the sequencer, now and in the future, and how many tracks you will probably need. If you are only interested in recording your practice sessions on a digital piano, the whole multitrack aspect of sequencing is irrelevant, and two tracks are enough (though in other ways a budget model may not be acceptable). If you have only a single keyboard but plan to expand your system with additional tone modules, eight tracks would be ample for the present, but perhaps a frustrating limitation in the future.

The question of tracks goes beyond merely considering how many voices and multitimbral parts your system contains. Because many sequencers allow for track merging, even a two-track unit could conceivably accomplish a complex recording in a large system. Conversely, someone working in a one-keyboard system might want an abundance of tracks for saving alternate "takes" of different parts. If you will be working with a drum machine or percussion module, remember that it can be convenient to isolate each percussion instrument part (hi-hat, snare, woodblock, etc.) on its own track for editing.

How many notes will the sequencer hold?

All sequencers have a memory ceiling that limits the number of recorded notes that can be held at once. Be careful when shopping, because this ceiling is sometimes defined in terms of events, and an event is not the same as a note. In fact, any note will consist of at least two MIDI events: the note-on and note-off commands. When a sequencer's specifications promise a 20,000-event capacity, you can count on recording 10,000 notes, at the most, before running out of room.

Actually it's not even that simple. Key movements are not the only events that you will generate. Any controller activity, such as depressing and releasing a sustain pedal, is an event. Furthermore, continuous controllers such as pitch-bend wheels, that generate a continuous stream of smoothly changing controller values, consume memory at a surprising rate. A single note that is bent upward and then down again before being released can encompass hundreds of events.

Does the sequencer have a disk drive?

If your sequencer doesn't include a disk drive, and if you want to save what you create, you may be sorely inconvenienced. Sequencers are essentially specialized computers, and like general-purpose computers they require an external place to store information when the internal memory is cleared out. Computers use floppy disks (and hard disks) for this purpose, and some sequencers also have floppy-disk drives built in. With these machines, it is possible to save to disk a piece you've been working on, load a different piece that was previously stored on a disk, and later reverse the process to continue working on the first piece.

What if there is no disk drive? In the worst case, you would have to erase forever whatever music is in the internal memory in order to begin something new. But it's not usually that grim. Most diskless sequencers contain a cassette interface for storing sequences on a standard cassette tape. (This interface is merely a plug on the back of the sequencer; you need to provide a cassette recorder and a tape.) Remember, you are not recording musical sound on the cassette; you are recording binary data which, if played back on a hi-fi system, would sound like a high-pitched squawk. When played back into the sequencer, however, your saved sequence is reestablished in its internal memory. Cassette data storage is much slower and more cumbersome than disks.

What editing features does the sequencer offer?

Sequencing power means editing power. Editing power is the ability to change musical data after it has been recorded. This question may seem a bit too general, even vague, and asking a music store salesperson, "How powerful is this sequencer?" may yield a glib response such as, "Oh, very." Here are some specifics to look for.

Sequencers perform their editing chores on three levels: the track level, the measure level, and the note (or event) level. The more detailed the changes can be (that is, the closer you can get to event-level editing), the more powerful will be your control over your data.

Track-level editing includes several basic functions. Some involve deleting whole tracks of data, or moving them to different tracks. This can be done as a "move," wherein the information is removed from one track and placed on another, or as a "copy," which places the data on a second track while leaving it on the first as well. An important track-level function allows merging of two recorded tracks, so that different musical parts are consolidated onto one track.

The pertinent question to ask is: "Can each sequencer track contain data recorded on more than one MIDI channel?" If so, you will be able to combine different parts—recorded on different tracks using different instrument settings—onto the same track, and they will play back with their respective channel assignments intact, so you will hear the correct instrument for each part. Some sequencers permanently connect each track to a MIDI channel, so that any data placed on that track will assume that channel and play back using whatever sound is assigned to the channel in your keyboard. This can lead to surprising results, and makes track merging much less useful, if it is possible at all. Here's another question to ask about merging: "Can tracks be unmerged?" This is done by extracting data of one MIDI channel and placing it back on its own track (or deleting it).

Other track-level functions involve leaving the data where it is but changing it somehow. Basic alterations include transposing, which moves all the pitches up or down by a specified number of notes; quantizing, which regulates rhythmic inconsistencies by aligning every note to the nearest beat or subbeat; changing velocity values to make a track softer or louder; stripping data, by which certain types of data (a particular pitch range, for example, or sustain-pedal information) are removed from the track, leaving the rest intact; changing duration, which alters the length of all notes in the track; or changing the MIDI channel of the entire track.

Any track-level function will probably be available on a measure-by-measure basis as well, assuming the sequencer implements editing by the measure. If so, you will be able to specify a range of measures (usually just one group of contiguous measures at a time) with data that you want to change. Some sequencers will permit you to choose whether the editing command will affect data within those measures on all tracks or just one. That kind of flexibility is an example of what makes some sequencers more powerful than others in ways that are not obviously apparent.

The most powerful sequencers are the ones that allow you to reach into your sequence and change the characteristics of individual notes. As with other editing levels, you should be able to change the MIDI channel, velocity, duration, pitch, and placement of the note.

Is it a pattern sequencer?

Because sequencers are often used for contemporary song writing, on both the commercial and recreational levels, some sequencers are designed for composing and recording within the formulas of modern song structures: that is to say, music that contains some combination of verses, choruses, bridges, and instrumental solos. Because the underlying tracks in a song structure tend to repeat themselves (from one verse to another, for example), it can be helpful to have a sequencer that is biased toward the use of patterns of music, which can be strung together in different combinations in the construction of a song.

This is not to say that this type of sequencer cannot be used in a more free-flowing manner, but because much of its operational savvy is given over to the storage and manipulation of patterned material, it really is the choice for people who primarily want to write songs.

What is the sequencer's range of tempos and time signatures?

Most music in our culture is written in a medium range of tempos and to a standard time signature of two, three, four, or six beats per measure. Because of this predominance, some sequencers do not extend much beyond the norm in these categories. If you prefer unusual meters, or simply want to be free to experiment, be sure to check to see if the sequencer is flexible and open-ended in assigning tempo and rhythm values. A tempo range of forty to 300 beats per minute should satisfy any need; for the time signature, you should be able to set the upper number between one and sixteen, and the bottom number should be able to represent half notes, quarter notes, eighth notes, and sixteenth notes. With this capability, the sequencer will allow time signature settings between 1⁄2 (one half note per measure, very unusual) and 16⁄16 (sixteen sixteenth notes per measure, likewise rare).

What is the sequencer's timing resolution?

All sequencers have an internal metronome that counts off the beats of each measure, either silently or audibly. Furthermore, this internal timing source divides time into much smaller segments (called "clocks" or "ticks") that determine the resolution with which musical data is recorded and played back. This resolution is usually defined by the number of ticks per quarter note. (This is called "pulses per quarter," or "ppq.") That is, how many minibeats does the sequencer's clock mark off between every quarter-note beat? (This number remains the same regardless of tempo. And don't worry, you can't hear these ticks.)

This is important because incoming data can only be placed (recorded) on one of these ticks, never between them. So, for example, if the sequencer only marks off two ticks between each quarter note (an impossibly low exaggeration) every note not exactly synchronized with these infrequent ticks would be pulled forward or back to the nearest tick. The playback would sound crazily distorted, with runs of notes clumped together onto available clocks like chords.

A resolution of ninety-six clocks per quarter note may be acceptable, but going any lower is not recommended for accurate recording. A common standard is 240 clocks, and this is ample for smooth, realistic recordings.

How does the sequencer's metronome work?

A steadily clicking (or blinking) metronome can be indispensable when recording the first tracks of a piece, but can turn into an annoyance if you must listen to its relentless timekeeping after you no longer need it.

Virtually all sequencers have metronomes, but they differ in how they can be used. Ideally, you would be able to set the metronome to automatically work only when you want it to: either during recording only, during playback, always, never, or only to count off a measure or two before recording.

Is the sequencer easy to use (user-friendly)?

Digital friendliness is a computer-age concept that refers to the user interface. This includes the machine's front panel, buttons, and screens—whatever bridges the gap between you and the actual operating system that records, edits, and plays back. This interface is considered friendly if it enables the user to learn how to access all the equipment's various features with minimal cursing, and without throwing the thing out of the window in frustration.

Although the friendliness factor can (and should) be applied to every MIDI component, it is unfortunately one of the hardest qualities to determine before purchasing. But here are a few things to watch for.

Generally, the more buttons a sequencer has, the friendlier it is, though a front panel bristling with controls may look hostile at first. If a sequencer is all clean lines and uncluttered surfaces, it means that whatever buttons are there have different functions in different situations, and their use will be more difficult to learn.

The bigger the information screen, the more information it will convey. A thirty-two-character screen is small but adequate; any smaller, and the sequencer may have to resort to cryptic language and strange symbols to tell you what you're doing or are about to do. Unfriendly.

Many sequencers are designed to resemble tape recorders, because that is familiar ground for most people. If you like that idea, look for the friendly play, stop, pause, rewind, and fast forward buttons featured on some equipment.

20
Software Sequencers

Product Profile

As computers have become more and more commonplace, software sequencing has also proliferated. Many programs have been developed for each of the four major platforms: IBM (MS-DOS), Macintosh, Atari, and Amiga.

Software sequencers generally fall into three price categories:

- Free public-domain programs.
- Less sophisticated commercial programs ($75 to $200).
- Fanciest professional programs ($250 to $600).

This is about the same range as hardware sequencers.

Summary of Shopping Questions

1. How many tracks does the sequencer offer?
2. How much memory does the program require?
3. What kind of graphic representation does the program offer?
4. Does the program include MIDI mixing?
5. Does the program support group soloing and group muting?
6. What are the program's quantizing options?
7. Is the program copy protected?
8. Does the software offer an undo feature?
9. Can the program exchange system-exclusive information with the rest of the system?
10. Does the software support more than sixteen MIDI channels?

How many tracks does the sequencer offer?

As with hardware sequencers, this is a good place to begin your evaluation. The answer to the question, though, will most likely be different, because software sequencing generally offers more tracks to work with than hardware units do. Sixteen seems to be a minimum, and some ambitious programs boast hundreds. How many is too many? Most people don't use more than about thirty, though it can be convenient to have a surplus, particularly if you like to record many different versions of the same part, and save them all for a while, each on its own track, until finally deciding which one is best. Also, it is a standard practice in MIDI production to isolate every percussion and drum part on its own track, even though many of them are assigned to the same MIDI channel. This way it is easy to mute one of those tracks to see what a passage would sound like without, say, the cowbell part. Because percussion parts can be busy and complex, this technique uses lots of tracks quickly.

How much memory does the program require?

This question is not as important if you have a large amount of RAM memory in your computer, but if you have less than two megabytes, it is a significant indicator of how much memory you'll have left over for your sequences. Whereas a hardware sequencer has an inherent memory limit of a certain number of MIDI events, with soft sequencing the limit is not inherent in the program, but in the computer. If your computer is equipped with 1 megabyte of RAM (1,000 kilobytes) and you have purchased a sequencer that requires 650 kilobytes to function, you have 350 kilobytes left over for music. This may be ample for your sequencing needs, but may not allow for additional RAM activity, such as ramdisks, multitasking, or many desk accessories.

The question depends in part on what kind of music and playing style will be recorded. The chief consideration is whether continuous controllers—devices such as pitch-bend wheels, modulation wheels, and joysticks that generate a stream of MIDI events—will be used extensively. These controllers consume memory ravenously and can inflate the size (in kilobytes; not in length) of a sequence very quickly.

What kind of graphic representation does the program offer?

The program's graphics should be easy to read and not be confusing. There is sometimes a trade-off here, as in other areas of technology, between power and ease of use. With software in particular, complicated and feature-laden programs can appear impenetrable and intimidating, while environments that look more "transparent" are sometimes actually a bit empty. Assuming you can spend some time trying different programs before buying, look for a balance of power and friendliness that appeals to you.

Here are some features that are useful in a software- sequencer program. Will the program allow you to place the windows in the most convenient arrangement and then save that configuration so the program boots up that way every time? How are notes represented? If you read music, you might want to look for a program that offers standard notation display, where the notes appear on music staves as in sheet music. Does the software present note data a few different ways, such as in notation, in piano-roll style, and as an event listing?

Does the program include MIDI mixing?

MIDI mixing is a feature that simulates an audio mixing board. In a professional multitrack recording studio, the tape deck plays back through a mixer, which is used to control each track of music separately. Each track is routed through its own channel (don't confuse these with MIDI channels; we're just on a side trip here) that is controlled by a sliding lever—a fader—that regulates the volume of the track in relation to all the others. Some sequencers have a window with a representation of mixer faders that can be assigned to recorded tracks. It is possible to record fader movements—and therefore volume changes on that track—as part of the sequence. Without these faders, it is still possible to accomplish volume changes (crescendos and decrescendos, for example), but it is not nearly as convenient. (Yet another side note: it is not actually the sequencer that is playing louder or softer. The sequencer is making appropriate adjustments to the velocity levels within the affected portion of the track, or, alternatively, it is controlling the synth with MIDI controller #7, which affects MIDI volume.)

Does the program support group soloing and group muting?

Professional mixers allow the engineer to solo a single channel so that only the track passing through that channel is heard (it turns all the others off), and also to mute a single channel so it is the only one not heard. Most software sequencers can do the same thing with their tracks (though it should be emphasized again that a mixer channel has nothing to do with a MIDI channel). Recording engineers can go a step further on most mixers by selecting a group of channels to solo or mute. This is tremendously useful when trying to mix a few parts with each other without the distraction of hearing everything else that has been recorded, and also when deciding whether a group of parts will be kept or erased. Group soloing and muting is just as useful in a sequencer.

What are the program's quantizing options?

Quantizing is an editing function that regulates the timing of events, and its purpose is to even out rhythmic irregularities. Let's say you have recorded a quickly moving bass part in which you intend there to be a note on every sixteenth-note beat. You may discover upon playback that the timing did not come out very accurately; some notes are slightly ahead of the beat, others slightly behind. Frankly, the track is a mess, but it's no problem. You can simply quantize the part to the sixteenth-note, and the timing of the track will be instantly perfect.

Unfortunately, perfect timing in music doesn't always sound natural, and a well-implemented quantizing function can help keep your sequences from sounding too mechanical. In addition to being able to select the fraction of a beat as a quantization value, look for an intensity regulator that you can use to soften the rigidity of a quantized part. For example, setting the intensity at 85 percent would align the notes to the nearest sixteenth note, but with an element of random placement equaling 15 percent. Some sequencers also have "humanizing" functions that correct the problem of overzealous quantizing. This is kind of a reverse quantization that randomizes perfectly timed notes. You should be able to set the degree of randomization here, too. Finally, look at whether a sequencer allows you to quantize both while you're playing and after the fact.

Is the program copy protected?

Copyright law attempts to protect the creator of a piece of software just as it protects the author of a book or the producer of a recording. This means it is illegal to copy software and distribute it, just as it is to make cassette copies of a CD and give them away (or, needless to say, to sell them). While there is no practical way to enforce this restriction when it comes to compact discs, computer software companies have a few tricks at their disposal. It is possible to embed software routines on the sequencer disk that actually make it impossible to successfully copy the program. While this protects the manufacturers from software theft, it is also a legitimate inconvenience to many users who want to make backup copies, as well as copies for their hard disks and ramdisks. Striking a middle ground, some companies allow a certain number of backup and operational copies to be made before the copy protection clamps down. Others, trying to stem a tide of negative customer relations, abstain from copy protection altogether. Yet another approach is to protect the program disk and invite registered customers to order additional protected copies from the manufacturer for a nominal fee. Still another solution is a hardware or software "key," included with the program, enabling the owner to run the program or any copies of the program.

Does the software offer an undo feature?

Nothing quite matches the horror of spending half the night recording the perfect piano part for your new song, and then accidentally deleting it. An undo option, which reverses the most recent editing operation, saves the day (or the night). It offers the additional benefit of allowing you to toggle between a newly edited version and the previous version of a part. So, for example, if you'd like to compare a quantized drum part with the unquantized version, you can switch back and forth between them using undo until you've decided which one is best.

Can the program exchange system-exclusive information with the rest of the system?

In any MIDI system, even within any MIDI component, there is a great deal of non-MIDI data activity. All keyboards and tone modules process information that helps them accomplish the internal business of creating, storing, and playing sounds. This is called system-exclusive (often shortened to "sysex") data, because it is exclusive to that particular keyboard. (In this context, the word "system" does not refer to a MIDI system of components, but to the operating system within a single component.)

Included in this information is patch data, the settings that tell the keyboard's envelopes, filters, and oscillators what sound to make; bank data, cataloging the order in which those patches are stored; the MIDI channel assignments; and the various global keyboard settings. This entire packet of information—essentially the entire internal contents of the keyboard or sound module—can be sent through MIDI cables as a single lump of data. This is unglamorously called a "system-exclusive dump."

It is convenient if the software can save a sysex dump either as part of a sequence or to a disk. This way, when you load a certain sequence into your program, you can also perform a sysex dump back into your keyboard and tone modules, configuring them instantly and automatically with the correct sounds and settings.

Does the software support more than sixteen MIDI channels?

If your computer requires an external MIDI interface (which it certainly does unless it's an Atari), and that interface has one MIDI IN jack and one MIDI OUT jack, you have access to the sixteen channels that are specified within MIDI. This may seem like enough at first. But if you acquire a few tone modules, each of which is multitimbral, it's easy to see how the original sixteen channels could be confining.

To get around this limitation, some MIDI interfaces are equipped with multiple INs and OUTs. Because each pair of MIDI jacks (one IN and one OUT) represents sixteen channels, your channel capacity can be dramatically expanded, and with it your ability to access the different timbres of several tone modules.

However, the sequencer must be able to handle more MIDI channels also, by allowing you to specify which MIDI OUT port a track's data will be sent to.

21
Workstations

Product Profile

The last several years have seen a huge growth in the popularity of multipurpose keyboards. These are more than just instruments; they are complete music production systems. The workstation concept includes a keyboard with internal samples and synthesis controls, a drum machine, and a sequencer. It can also include a sampler, for example, but those are the basic elements. Workstations are basically integrated, self-contained, portable MIDI recording studios. The idea is to replace (or augment) the multicomponent setup of a traditional MIDI system.

The advantages are several. For one thing, it is very convenient to have everything you need in one package, right under your hands. It is easier to learn the features of a single workstation than a handful of separate pieces of hardware; the learning curve is gentler. And, for performing keyboardists who use sequenced material on stage, the portability is a great plus. All the necessary sounds, the sequences, the keyboard, and drum machine can fit into one case.

There are disadvantages also. When you choose a workstation, you lose the unique strengths that can be found in specialized components. Workstation sequencers tend to be less powerful than their hardware counterparts (though not necessarily), and certainly less so than software programs. Workstations, though each has its own strengths, tend to strive for good overall performance, rather than excelling in any particular area.

Many people have found them to be a smart first purchase, because they offer so much for the money. A workstation can help you get your feet wet in the areas of MIDI playing, programming, composing, and recording, often for not much more than the cost of a keyboard alone. MIDI consumers have now come to expect this cost effectiveness to such a degree that many, if not most, keyboards have sequencers onboard.

You should shop for a workstation considering many of the same issues as shopping for other keyboards. In this chapter, we'll focus on questions unique to workstations. It should also be noted that we are discussing only consumer workstations, not the very expensive digital powerhouses designed (and priced) only for the commercial studio.

Most workstations cost $1,000 to $3,000. An active used market has developed, thanks to the quick pace at which new instruments have been developed.

Summary of Shopping Questions

1. How many tracks can the sequencer use?
2. How powerful is the sequencer?
3. How big is the workstation's LCD?
4. How much memory does the sequencer contain?
5. What kind of external storage does the workstation offer?
6. Does the workstation feature onboard digital effects?
7. How many outputs does the workstation have?

How many tracks can the sequencer use?

The more, the better. All workstation recorders have at least eight tracks; many have sixteen; a very few have more. If you haven't owned a sequencer before, eight may seem like plenty, and indeed it might be enough. However, if the keyboard is sixteen-part multitimbral, it would be hard to take advantage of that feature with an eight-track sequencer.

How powerful is the sequencer?

This refers to the editing power of the sequencer, its ability to manipulate recorded data. Usually, workstation sequencers take a back seat to stand-alone units when it comes to editing features, but there are some basic abilities to watch for:

- Can you merge tracks? This will be especially important if there aren't that many tracks to work with, but it may not be possible if they are not multichannel tracks. Some workstations assign voices simultaneously to a MIDI channel and the corresponding sequencer track, and this assignment cannot be changed. If this is the case, the tracks probably cannot contain data on more than one channel and probably cannot be merged.

- Can the sequencer quantize individual tracks? Are different degrees of quantization available?
- Are there basic cut-and-paste functions? You should be able to cut a portion of a track and paste the cut data somewhere else. It's helpful to be able to paste it into another track.
- Can a track or a portion of a track be looped?
- Does the sequencer operate in pattern and linear modes? Some workstation sequencers can switch between pattern and linear operation.
- Can the sequencer edit individual events?
- Can an entire track be transposed?

How big is the workstation's LCD?

As always, the bigger the LCD screen, the better. This is especially true with any device that contains a sequencer.

How much memory does the sequencer contain?

This is usually measured in terms of note capacity. A sequencer that can hold 7,000 notes is small. Keep in mind that a note is not the same as a MIDI event. Occasionally, sequencer memory limits are listed by events, but every recorded note contains at least two events: a note-on and a note-off. So a 16,000-event sequencer would have, at most, an 8,000-note limit.

Another memory-related question is: how many songs can the sequencer hold in its memory? This is especially important for MIDI performers who use sequenced tracks on stage.

What kind of external storage does the workstation offer?

This is a good question when shopping for any keyboard but is especially important with workstations, because you'll need to save your sequences in addition to any banks of sound programs you create. All workstations will offer some kind of external storage, either a RAM card slot or a floppy-disk drive. (Sampling workstations often contain internal hard-disk drives for storing samples, which take up a great deal of memory.) You can also use a third-party disk archiver, a generic disk drive for storing all kinds of MIDI data (see chapter 16).

Does the workstation feature onboard digital effects?

If the workstation is truly to be an all-in-one production system, some basic processing effects are crucial, unless you already have an external (outboard) signal processor (like a reverb box).

How many outputs does the workstation have?

All workstations are equipped with at least a pair of stereo outputs. Some contain additional outputs to be connected to separate mixer channels. Different patches can be assigned to different outputs, giving you more control over the mix of your sequence. Of course, you need to have enough available input channels on your mixer to take advantage of multiple outputs.

22

Samplers

Product Profile

Samplers are the chameleons of the MIDI world. Unlike synthesizers, sample-playback keyboards, and other instruments that come loaded with their own sounds, samplers have no sonic individuality (no identifying sound of their own). In fact, they make no sound whatsoever until a sample is loaded into the internal memory. But they have a peculiar versatility in that they can record and play back any sound presented to them. Synthesizers are also capable of near-infinite variety, but they are limited to a certain selection of basic waveforms. All samplers may not have the same power as synthesizers in the sound-synthesis department, but there is no limit to the different waveforms you can work with. Simply plug in a microphone, record a sound, and you have a new patch. (Of course, the actual process of making a good, usable sample is sometimes a bit more complicated.)

Because of their unique features, samplers can be harder to shop for than other instruments. Because they don't have a factory bank of preset sounds, they are harder to demo in the store. For this reason it's especially important to understand the specifications of samplers—what they mean, and whether a certain feature is important to you. Many of the questions in this chapter will focus on these specifications.

Samplers, like synthesizers, are packaged both as keyboards and tone modules, though not every sampler will necessarily be available in both configurations. They vary widely in the power of their voice architecture. Some specialize in capturing high-quality samples at the expense of more complex synthesis controls; others offer more powerful voicing features. Voice architecture within a sampler—in addition to parameters that regulate the envelopes, filters, LFOs, and other tone modifiers— can refer to the specialized functions of looping, pitch-shifting, and cross-fading. These are operations performed on the sampled waveform that make it more realistic and playable from a keyboard.

Many people who buy samplers never use them to actually sample new wave- forms. They become simply sample-playback instruments. What is the advantage of having a sampler if you're not going to sample? The benefit is in the large libraries of prerecorded samples available for most popular models. Even if the audio input is never used, the open, unlimited architecture of a sampler is attractive to those who want endless variety in the sounds available to them. Taking advantage of this marketing niche, there is at least one model available in a less expensive, playback- only version. (It is not, strictly speaking, a sampler, but it has access to the same sample library.)

Because of their sophisticated recording and signal-processing functions, samplers are expensive. There's a very wide range; costs for new instruments are generally $1,500 to $10,000. The most popular models for recreational and semiprofessional use fall between $2,000 to $3,000. There is a fairly active used market, though people tend to be more reluctant to part with a sampler than a synthesizer, perhaps because the initial investment was greater.

Summary of Shopping Questions

The questions in this chapter focus on the qualities unique to samplers, as distinct from other keyboards. But because they are keyboard instruments (unless you're shopping for a sampling module), the basic MIDI control features should be considered also. For questions relating to them, see chapter 18.

1. Does the sampler include a sound library, and what is available for future purchase?
2. What kind of graphic display is on the sampler's front panel?
3. What is the sampler's bit resolution?
4. What sampling rates are available?
5. What is the sampler's maximum sample time?
6. What is the sampler's internal memory capacity, and is it expandable?
7. What sample-processing features does the sampler offer?
8. How powerful is the sampler's voice architecture?
9. What disk drives and interfaces are included with the sampler?

Does the sampler include a sound library, and what is available for future purchase?

As mentioned, samplers do not make a single sound until you put one into them. They are only usable with a library of sounds, which can either be built through custom sampling or purchased on disk. Many manufacturers (or the stores that represent them) will include a collection of samples in the purchase price of the equipment. They might come on floppy disks, or loaded onto the internal hard drive if there is one. Either way, their inclusion can be a price negotiating point on both sides. The question of a sound library is especially important, because it defines what the instrument can be and how it will suit your needs.

You might also want to explore what is available, or will be, in the future. The manufacturer is probably involved with developing a large library, and third-party developers might provide alternatives also. Think of these considerations:

- How extensive is the library available for this sampler?
- Does it suit your tastes and needs?
- Can library disks be auditioned and bought in the store, or are they only available through the mail?

The most important shopping activity is to audition as much of the library as possible. Samplers should not be purchased purely on the basis of their technical specifications. You are really auditioning the *software* (the sound library) as much as the hardware.

What kind of graphic display is on the sampler's front panel?

The user interface in general and the size of the LCD in particular are always considerations when looking at keyboards. It's especially important with samplers because of their capacity for waveform processing. In some cases, it is necessary to perform cutting, pasting, and looping operations on the actual waveform. It is very helpful to be able to see the shape of the wave itself. This requires a fairly large, graphic LCD.

Samplers offer a greater variety of choices in graphic interfaces than other keyboards. Some models offer a connection to an external monitor, turning the sampler into a specialized computer. Others have the standard LCD on the front panel, which can vary in size. This size is specified either by the number of characters that can be displayed, or by the number of pixels, like a computer monitor. (A pixel is a single graphic "dot" on a display screen.) Preferably, the screen will be of the graphic kind (measured in terms of pixels), but more often it will be a character display, and, in this case, the larger, the better. Twenty-two characters is on the small end of the scale; some LCDs can display as many as 320 characters. Alphanumeric (character) displays can only show words and numbers; graphic displays can show waveforms and other pictures.

What is the sampler's bit resolution?

When a sample is recorded or played back, it is "described" by a certain number of bits of information. The more bits, the more complete the "picture" of the sound wave will be (see chapter 7 for a complete discussion of bit resolution)

The standard resolution for compact disk fidelity is sixteen-bit. The first samplers to appear on the scene were eight-bit instruments; now they all process with twelve, sixteen, or more bits. When looking over specifications for samplers, you may see that different rates are listed. This is because the machine can use one level of resolution when recording the sample and another when playing it back. So there may be an ADC (analog-digital conversion) rate, and a DAC (digital-analog conversion) rate. There also might be an internal rate that defines the resolution used when processing the waveform within the sampler. Pay attention to the lowest rate listed, because it will define the quality and fidelity of the samples. So, if an instrument samples (ADC) at sixteen-bit, and has a DAC rate upon playback of twenty-bit, this simply means that the sixteen-bit sample is being "described" very accurately, but it is still just a sixteen-bit sample (which is a high-quality sample to begin with).

What sampling rates are available?

The other factor in determining how accurately a sampled waveform is represented digitally is the sample rate. This refers to the number of digital "snapshots" taken of the waveform every second (see chapter 7 for further discussion). The CD standard for sample rate is 44,100 "snapshots" per second (44.1 kHz).

The sample rate is variable in most samplers, although the 44.1 kHz rate is the standard. The rate you choose when sampling helps determine how much memory is available for storing the sample (see the next question). There is a huge range represented among samplers, from about 6 kHz to 60 kHz.

A higher sampling rate will generally deliver a more accurate reproduction of the sound being sampled, but the improvement is not heard across the board as it is with the bit resolution. Specifically, a high rate is required to capture high-frequency (pitch) sounds. So a cymbal crash, which has a great deal of high-frequency content, would only be accurately sampled with a high sampling rate; if a lower rate were used, some of the cymbal's sound would be lost. The CD standard of 44.1 kHz is high enough to capture most frequencies we can hear.

What is the sampler's maximum sample time?

This question refers to the longest sample (usually measured in seconds) that the internal memory can hold. As mentioned in the previous question, sample time is influenced by the chosen sample rate: higher sample rates shorten available memory. This makes sense, when you think that a higher sampling rate is taking more digital impressions of the sound wave every second, and therefore more memory is required for each second of recorded sound.

Sample times range from about five to ninety seconds, depending on these variables, and also by the amount of available RAM. The internal memory may also be expandable.

What is the sampler's internal memory capacity, and is it expandable?

A sampler's internal memory capacity affects the previous question, and also helps determine how many samples can be loaded simultaneously into the instrument. You may have realized by now that all the different aspects of sampler memory are interrelated. By and large, samplers contain one large block of RAM, which is allotted according to the length of the sample, how many samples need to be loaded, and the sample rate.

One half megabyte (500k) is at the small end of internal RAM. Some samplers come equipped off the shelf with eight megs, which is substantial. (A typical sample-playback synth is loaded with four megs of samples; some digital pianos have dozens of megs devoted to their instrument samples.) Internal sampler RAM is sometimes expandable by adding memory chips.

This is not to be confused with internal hard drives that are included with some samplers. The hard drive is for storage of sounds not currently being used; they are loaded from the hard drive into RAM.

What sample-processing features does the sampler offer?

When a sample is first recorded it is "raw," and probably not very playable. That is to say, it cannot convincingly imitate the original instrument when controlled from a keyboard. Raw samples are often not musically realistic until they are treated in various ways. The power and ease with which the sampler accomplishes this is an important consideration.

The most crucial treatment of a raw sample is usually looping. Samples are by definition short, but most music requires longer, sustained tones. Looping a sample is a way of extending its length without taking up any more valuable memory. At the most basic level, it works like a tape loop. When the sample reaches the end of its playing time, it simply repeats. In this way the sampled tone can last as long as a key is held down.

If that were all there is to it, looping would be easy. But a simple repeating loop does not always yield effective results. Loops are only convincing when they cannot be heard. When you consider that a sampled tone is almost never played at exactly the same tone or intensity at the end of the sample as it was at the beginning, it is easy to see that a loop that skips instantaneously from one end to the other would sound strange. A "bad loop" of a short sample has a kind of rhythmic, pulsing effect, which is definitely not desirable.

More sophisticated looping alternatives are usually provided, and the more options a sampler offers in this department, the more persuasive and satisfying its samples will be. Sometimes variable loop points can be assigned, so that the loop "ends" can be as close to identical in tone as possible. Forward and backward looping is fairly common. Some machines support an autofind feature, with which the sampler will calculate the optimum loop points and create the best loop for you.

Other digital processing besides looping includes compression and expansion of the sample, merging of two samples, and splicing of one sample into another. Here's where a large, friendly graphic interface comes in handy!

Keep in mind that all these processing features are important only for custom sampling. Purchased library samples come preprocessed and ready to play.

How powerful is the sampler's voice architecture?

Most samplers are equipped, to some degree, with synthesizer-type sound-creation abilities. The difference is that the sampler can acquire its own original, raw waveforms as building blocks. Because a sampler's primary purpose is to record and play new waveforms, its voice architecture is not always as powerful as in a dedicated synthesizer. Still, any instrument must sound good to be useful and fun, and some kind of basic voice control helps. Look for these basic features:

- Envelope control over the volume (amplitude) of a sample. How many stages does the envelope have? Four is a working minimum. Envelopes that control the pitch and tone of the sample are also useful.

- Filters can soften the rough edges of a sample or brighten a dull one. Low-pass and high-pass filters are most common; resonance filters are less typical.

- LFO (low-frequency oscillator) contributes expressive effects such as vibrato and tremolo.

What disk drives and interfaces are included with the sampler?

Unlike other types of keyboards and tone modules, samplers always contain some kind of disk-based external storage. Digital samples are simply too big to fit on RAM and ROM cards, and take up too much internal memory to be stored there indefinitely. Floppy-disk drives that use either high-density or double-density disks are common. Sometimes the sampler will have an internal hard disk, which adds a much larger amount of storage capacity; sometimes the hard disk is an option that can be installed later. Some models also have an interface next to the MIDI jacks for connecting an external hard drive or a CD-ROM player.

It should be noted that when we speak of an internal hard drive, we are still referring to external storage, since the samples are being removed from RAM and stored somewhere else.

23

Drum Machines

Product Profile

Drum machines have evolved tremendously over the last ten years. Some older models are still prized for their classic sound, while newer rhythm machines are valued for their realism, range of sounds, and sequencing features.

Drum machines have evolved into two basic categories, each useful in its own way. On one hand, there are the traditional desktop models with drum pads, preset patterns, and a pattern-based sequencer for recording new rhythms. For years these were popular with "one-person-band" keyboard players who used these devices to accompany themselves. More recently, we've seen the development of the percussion module, which is designed to be used in a sequencing environment. These devices are usually rack-mounted, and their sounds are accessed with a keyboard, just like any other tone module.

Prices for new drum machines and modules span the $200 to $3,500 range, with the most popular ones costing between $400 and $1,000.

Summary of Shopping Questions

1. Do you want a traditional drum machine or a percussion module?
2. How many pads does the drum machine have, and are they velocity sensitive?
3. How many sounds does the drum machine/module offer, and are they the correct sounds for your needs?

4. How flexible are the machine's/module's editing functions?

5. How many audio outputs does the machine/module include?

6. What is the equipment's bit resolution?

7. What is the equipment's polyphony?

8. Does the drum machine/module accept new waveforms?

9. What is the equipment's timing resolution?

10. What is the equipment's time signature range?

11. What is the equipment's memory capacity?

12. Can patterns, songs, and kits be stored externally?

13. Can the drum machine synchronize to an external timing source?

14. Does the drum machine have a footswitch jack, and what does it do?

15. Does the drum machine offer "feel" features?

Do you want a traditional drum machine or a percussion module?

The answer to this question depends on how you plan to use the drum machine. The traditional approach gives you the ability (though it doesn't require you) to work on the machine itself. You can access its drum sounds from the front panel drum pads, and you can create new rhythm patterns using the internal sequencer. If you need to make your rhythms portable, the traditional drum machine is the way to go, because it's completely self-contained. Also if you don't have a sequencer and don't plan on getting one soon, you need the traditional model. Traditional drum machines often offer a greater selection of preset rhythm patterns than percussion modules, which is a consideration if you want an instrument that is immediately useful, right out of the box, in a wide range of applications.

One advantage to getting a percussion module is that, because it's rack mounted, you don't need to give up valuable surface space to accommodate one. Aside from this logistic benefit, percussion modules are better suited to working in sequencing environments. Because their internal memory is not taken up with sequencing software and as many preset patterns as traditional machines, there is more room for drum and percussion samples. Some of these modules contain hundreds of high-quality, realistic drum sounds. However, because the user interface (without the drum pads) is not as friendly, and because you will need to establish a keyboard map (keymap) to access the sounds, the learning curve is a little steeper with these modules. Most percussion modules come equipped with several preset keymaps that give you a number of keyboard-based drum kits ready to go.

If you can't decide which type of drum machine to purchase, it might be best to go with the traditional style, because they can be used as percussion modules by disregarding the drum pads and the internal sequencer, whereas percussion modules cannot be used in a traditional way.

How many pads does the drum machine have, and are they velocity sensitive?

Traditional drum machines enable you to assign a different sound to each of the different pads. In this way, you can construct a drum kit that can be played from the front panel of the machine. Naturally, the more pads there are, the larger the kit can be, and the more options you'll have in selecting sounds.

These pads can be touch sensitive (velocity sensitive), so that the harder you hit a pad, the louder the assigned drum sounds will be. This adds immeasurably to the realistic expressiveness of the drum machine. However, not all drum pads are velocity sensitive. Confusing the matter somewhat is the fact that the sounds themselves *can* be velocity sensitive, even if the pads are not. This means that if you're using the drum machine as a percussion module, controlling the sounds from a velocity- sensitive MIDI keyboard, the internal drum samples will respond to the velocity data (in other words, how hard you're hitting the keys), but they will not do so when you're using the drum machine's own pads.

How many sounds does the drum machine/module offer, and are they the correct sounds for your needs?

As with any digital instrument, the more the better. Think of sixty-four preset samples as a minimum. However, sometimes it's better to invest in an instrument with fewer sounds if they are just the *right* sounds for your tastes and needs.

Some drum machines specialize in rendering "bread-and-butter" drum-kit samples usually heard in popular music. These might include hi-hats, crash cymbals, ride cymbals, snares, toms and floor toms, kick drums, cowbells, and rim shots; a few other percussion sounds might be thrown in. Often these machines are not highly programmable, so that the samples cannot be heavily processed to create new sounds. Their purpose is simply to emulate standard drum kits.

Although all drum machines contain standard drum samples, some provide more unusual instruments as well and a greater capacity for creating new percussion sounds. The more unusual instruments could include congas, various shakers, woodblocks, bells, chimes, and ethnic percussion instruments from around the world. In addition, some modules contain basic synthetic waveforms from which you can create original percussive timbres.

Some percussion machines contain nonpercussion sounds. Bass is particularly common. Bass and drums together comprise the traditional rhythm section of most popular music. The bass sample is tunable and assignable to the pads just like any other onboard sound. Of course, it is much easier to use this type of drum machine, when controlling it from a keyboard, by assigning each bass note to its corresponding key. Other nonpercussion sounds might be special effects such as breaking glass or human voice samples.

How flexible are the machine's/module's editing functions?

Like synthesizers, most drum machines allow some sound-shaping control over the samples. Here are a few basic features to watch for.

Transposition is one of the most useful parameters. To transpose is to change the pitch. Although most percussion sounds are not "pitched" in the same way as melody instruments (like flutes or violins), the samples can still be transposed in exactly the same way. Doing so can create some extraordinary effects. Usually the sounds can be transposed in half-step increments. You should at least be able to transpose drum sounds up and down by three or four half-steps for fine tuning. It will also give you enough flexibility to deepen the sound of a bass drum, or raise the pitch of a woodblock to match the key of a song. Some percussion machines enable transposition within a range of a few octaves, and here the results can be dramatic. Transpose a crash cymbal down by twenty-four half steps, for example, and suddenly you have a gong. Or lower a floor tom by the same amount and it sounds like a huge Japanese traditional drum, or perhaps something less recognizable. Experimenting with this feature can yield powerful and unexpected sounds and effects.

Decay is another basic parameter, referring to the time a sound takes to fade. Using this setting, a crash cymbal that would normally ring for a few seconds can be shortened; a snare drum that has a bit too much ringing after its fundamental hit can be clipped to include only the sound desired.

Another method of creating sounds, used by some drum machines, is to stack samples on top of each other. Combining different instruments so that they are all "hit" at the same time can yield some powerful and unusual sounds.

How many audio outputs does the machine/module include?

The number of audio outputs is important in a studio situation in which all the signals from various modules and keyboards are fed into a mixer. In this arrangement, every mixer channel, representing an output from a sound source, can be treated differently. The sound source can be placed in the stereo image (panning) and processed with digital effects such as reverb. With any sound module (like a drum machine) that can produce different sounds simultaneously, it is helpful to separate each sound onto its own channel as much as possible. This gives you much more control in mixing all the parts together. The more outputs there are, naturally, the greater the separation. All drum machines will have at least a stereo pair of outputs. Some will have between two and eight additional outputs. By assigning different sounds to different outputs and running them all into a mixer (assuming you have enough mixer inputs), you can change the volume levels, panning positions, and reverb treatments of each percussion instrument separately. This is similar to miking a live drum set with highly directional microphones on each drum and cymbal.

What is the equipment's bit resolution?

Every sample is created and then read (played back) according to a certain resolution, which is defined by the number of bits that are contained in the playback description. The greater the number of bits, the more accurate the description of the sample will be, and the more convincing it will sound to the ear. Sixteen-bit resolution is the standard for CD-quality sound reproduction.

There are two parts to the recording process to consider when shopping for drum machines. The sample resolution refers to the number of bits that were used when recording the onboard drum samples, while the DAC (digital-analog conversion) resolution refers to the number of bits available when the machine is translating the digital sample into an analog sound signal. The lower number of these two rates will determine the sound that actually reaches your ears. The DAC-bit resolution is sometimes higher, but this just means that the original sample is being described very well and accurately. Its fidelity is still limited by whatever limitations are inherent in the original sample. Most current-model drum machines contain sixteen-bit samples, and sound quite realistic and clean.

What is the equipment's polyphony?

As with a synthesizer, polyphony is an important consideration, though drum machines are less likely to experience problems with insufficient polyphony than keyboards. There are two reasons for this. First, most drum sounds are quite short and are therefore only using up a voice very briefly. This is different from a keyboard or tone module creating long, sustained tones that might get cut off if their polyphony is exceeded. Second, realistic drum programming doesn't usually call for many drums to be sounding at the same time. So eight-voice polyphony might be perfectly acceptable in a drum machine, though it would be spartan for a keyboard.

Keep in mind that if a drum machine offers voice layering, and if you plan to use that feature, the polyphony will be reduced. The range for polyphony is between five and thirty-two voices.

Does the drum machine module accept new waveforms?

Sometimes the factory samples that come with a drum machine may not be sufficient for your needs, or your needs may change. Many manufacturers offer libraries of new samples on ROM cards that simply plug into the drum machine. There is not as much third-party development of drum-machine libraries as there is with keyboard sounds and samples; these cards are mostly available from the manufacturers themselves.

Another possibility, albeit a high-end one, is to consider a drum machine with a sampling option. However, this is a much more expensive alternative, and creating effective samples is much more difficult than buying them.

What is the equipment's timing resolution?

Timing resolution is crucial because realistic rhythm tracks sometimes depend on subtly imprecise timing, and a high timing resolution is required to obtain that. When the metronome is on, we only hear the main beats, but the internal software is generating many smaller divisions of time into which we can place percussion events. If those divisions of time are too few the rhythm patterns can sound mechanical and stilted, because every played note is placed on the nearest subbeat, which may not be exactly when it was played.

The timing resolution is usually given as pulses per quarter note (ppq), and ninety-six ppq is standard. Sometimes it will be referred to differently, as a note value (sixteenth note or thirty-second note). Machines that list their timing resolution in note values usually lack enough flexibility for most players. This becomes obvious when you consider that a sixteenth note resolution is equal to four ppq.

What is the equipment's time signature range?

The time signature defines how many of what kind of note is in each measure. That may be a trifle confusing. As an example, a piece in 4/4 time contains four quarter notes in each measure. A 6/8 piece has measures that contain six eighth notes each. Some time signatures are much more common than others, with 4/4 being the hands-down winner in the realm of Western popular music. If your musical needs are not esoteric, then almost any drum machine may be satisfactory in this regard.

But if you like to experiment with odd time signatures (or if you think you might like to sometime), you'd do well to check the machine's ability to be flexible with time. Some machines won't allow a 9/8 time signature, for example, or 5/4. Some are accommodating with the top number, but limited in the bottom number. Percussion modules without sequencers will, of course, not list any specification for time signatures.

What is the equipment's memory capacity?

If you are looking at a drum machine with a sequencer, check the number of notes that can be recorded. This is not always listed, but when it is, it will range from about 2,500 notes on the low end up to about 60,000.

Check the number of patterns that can be stored in the machine. In most cases, patterns are the building blocks for the rhythm parts of whole songs. Try to determine whether you'll be creating many of your own patterns or relying mostly on the factory patterns. The memory for the preset patterns is in ROM, and different from the user-available pattern memory, which is in RAM. It's good to have 100 pattern slots for your own storage needs; some machines offer many fewer and some many more.

A related memory concern is the number of songs that can be stored. Because a song is usually a larger entity than a pattern, there are correspondingly fewer song memory slots in most machines, ranging from eight to a few hundred. The question of how many songs can fit into the machine at one time is especially important if the drum machine will be used in a live playing setting where it will be providing the rhythm section for an evening's worth of songs. The question becomes crucial if external storage is a problem (see the following question).

The final internal memory consideration is how many drum kits can be stored at once. Most models are equipped with factory preset kits, in which different drum sounds are grouped together, assigned to the pads, and available at the same time for composing. In addition you can create your own kits and store them to memory. The number of user-available memory slots ranges from one to over 100.

All these categories can be affected if the drum machine uses RAM expansion cards. These plug right into the unit and can double the amount of memory available for notes, patterns, songs, and kits.

Can patterns, songs, and kits be stored externally?

The most common format with which drum machine data is stored externally is via a system-exclusive data dump. By means of a sysex dump, a drum machine's patterns, kits, songs, and sequences can be saved to an external device such as a MIDI disk drive or a computer.

Drum machines, like keyboards, also use RAM cards, which are convenient but relatively expensive, and disk drives to store information. Having a built-in disk drive is the most cost-effective storage medium in the long run, particularly if you'll be saving a lot of data, but it will add significantly to the purchase cost of the instrument. If the drum machine contains none of these options, it probably offers a cassette-storage interface. This enables you to hook up a cassette recorder to the drum machine and save your data to standard analog cassettes. This is inexpensive, but extremely slow and inconvenient.

Can the drum machine synchronize to an external timing source?

This question is relevant only for certain applications. Some people prefer to create their rhythm patterns on the drum machine itself, using the internal sequencer, and then use those patterns as part of a sequence that has been created on another sequencer. In this case, it is essential to control both sequencers with just one timing source (metronome), so that they will synchronize exactly. Because the other, full-featured sequencer is likely to have better control features, it makes sense to use it as the metronome. So the internal "conductor" of the drum machine must be turned off, and it must be set to receive its timing commands over MIDI.

This is not a problem for most drum machines with sequencers. You will find that there are a variety of timing protocols that are accepted or not accepted. The most basic is MIDI clocks, which is all you need to slave the drum machine to another sequencer. The others refer to time codes that can be recorded to a multitrack tape deck or video editing deck when sequenced material needs to be synchronized to tape recorded tracks or video. They are Song Position Pointer (SPP), SMPTE (a standard developed by the Society of Motion Picture and Television Engineers), and MIDI Time Code (MTC, not the same as MIDI clocks).

Does the drum machine have a footswitch jack, and what does it do?

Because drum machines are often used to accompany live performances, a footswitch is often included, enabling you to control certain functions without using your hands. Sometimes the footswitch will have only one function, such as triggering a note, and sometimes the function is programmable. Other useful options include: starting and stopping the sequencer, selecting a drum kit, retriggering a pattern, establishing a tempo by tapping on the footswitch, ending a repeating section, controlling the open/closed position of a hi-hat sample, advancing to the next pattern in a song.

Does the drum machine offer "feel" features?

It is hard to control a drum machine with the same precision as a drummer can play a real drum kit. To compensate for this, many drum patterns are heavily quantized, which eliminates rhythmic irregularities. Unfortunately, perfectly timed patterns rarely sound natural, and can even be as unrealistic as sloppily timed patterns. To strike some middle ground between imprecision and sterility, many drum modules are equipped with software algorithms that add certain "feels" to quantized patterns. This can be achieved with a subtle randomization of note timings, making the drum part sound more human. By selecting a swing-jazz feel, a straight eighth-note pattern can be transformed into the loping, dotted eighth-note sound of a jazz combo.

24

Home Keyboards and Digital Pianos

Product Profile

This chapter is devoted to questions that should be asked when shopping for a keyboard that doesn't fit into the professional category. Home keyboards, as they are called, range from small portable models costing under $200 to full-blown digital pianos in grand-piano style cabinets, costing thousands. This class of instrument also includes portable digital pianos. It should be noted that not all of the smaller, inexpensive models are MIDI instruments; this can always be determined by simply checking for the presence of MIDI jacks.

Typically, the portables have light, unweighted key actions, while the digital pianos have a weighted feel. This is to be expected, because digital pianos are trying to emulate their acoustic counterparts in every way.

The one distinguishing feature of home keyboards is built-in speakers. Home keyboards do not need external amplification to be heard, although most of them contain auxiliary outputs if such amplification is desired. Autoplay features are also characteristic—but not necessarily so—of home keyboards. This usually includes the automatic formation of accompaniment chords by playing a single left hand note, as well as rhythmic accompaniments. In some cases this includes sequencing capability, with which you can record your own autoplay rhythm and harmony patterns; or there may be only preset accompaniments without any recording facility.

The cost of home portable keyboards ranges between $150 and $2,500. Most digital pianos cost between $1,500 and $5,000.

Summary of Shopping Questions

1. How does the keyboard sound?
2. Is the keyboard's action weighted?
3. Is the keyboard easy to use?
4. How many keys does the keyboard have?
5. How many onboard sounds does the keyboard offer?
6. How many preset accompaniment patterns does the keyboard have?
7. What are the keyboard's autoplay functions?
8. Is the keyboard velocity sensitive?
9. Does the keyboard have a sequencer?
10. How much does the keyboard weigh?
11. Does the keyboard offer onboard effects?
12. Does the keyboard come with the necessary peripherals?
13. Does the keyboard accept external samples and rhythms?
14. Does the keyboard offer external storage?
15. Is the keyboard multitimbral?

How does the keyboard sound?

As always, this is the most important question when buying any instrument. Most portables carry the same range of instrument presets, at least when comparing models at the same general price point. But there is some variation in quality, and one model may sound much richer to you than another, even if they share the same basic features and factory selections. Check not only the instrument settings, but also the drum patterns, the individual drum sounds, and the accompaniment patterns. Most portable keyboards have demonstration songs stored in ROM memory. These show off the instrument in the best possible light and can be fun to listen to. Remember that creating a piece as complex as the demo may require more work and playing skill than you possess. A better gauge of the keyboard's actual sound would be to focus on the individual sounds and accompaniment patterns that you might use.

When shopping for a digital piano, overall sound is also crucial. Because you are looking for a digital version of an acoustic piano, it is obviously very important that you are pleased with the piano sample. Some instruments, hoping to cover all tastes, offer more than one piano setting, representing different samples. Many of the higher-end models also include some kind of tone-variation controls, such as equalization. This is a valuable feature, because it allows you to customize the sound to a degree. Listen closely to the decay of the sound. Can you hear the points where the sample has been artificially looped? This might be particularly evident if there is a strings program, because loops are most evident in the upper ranges. The best programs have inaudible loops. It's the sort of thing that may not be too obvious in the first listen at a busy (and noisy) music store, but which in the quiet of your home can prove annoying over time.

Is the keyboard's action weighted?

The way a keyboard sounds is kinesthetically related to the way it feels. A certain sample will actually sound more pleasing subjectively if the keyboard with which you are playing it feels good. This is primarily true for more experienced players, particularly if they are used to acoustic piano actions.

Portable pianos usually have unweighted keys. Digital pianos are often weighted, but each brand has its own feel and degree of resistance. The system known as "weighted hammer" action is the most costly, and perhaps most realistic, kind of heavy action. Another design is the "weighted/rotary oil-damped" action, which can also imitate a piano's feel. Some actions are very lightly weighted, which might be best for players without a strong background on the acoustic piano.

A weighted action is one of the most important requirements in a keyboard that will be used as a practice instrument for a beginning piano student. This is a popular use for these instruments, and most teachers will insist that their students practice on a weighted action. The reason is simple. If a beginning player becomes accustomed to the light, easy response of an unweighted action, playing an acoustic piano, with it's naturally heavy keys, will seem extremely difficult and unwieldy by comparison.

Is the keyboard easy to use?

Most portable home keyboards have rather complicated front panels, which can actually be an advantage when it comes to user-friendliness. The idea behind having many buttons and sliders is that almost every function will have a dedicated control. Once you learn where all the controls are and what they do, this is an easier arrangement than many professional keyboards, whose sleek and sparse layouts may require every button and slider to have multiple functions. Still, home keyboards can seem hopelessly complicated at first glance, and it's worth taking the time to learn your way around enough to know whether the keyboard will be easy to navigate. Try the autoplay features, switching from fingered mode to single-finger operation. If there are recording options, make sure they are clear. Move from one program, and one accompaniment preset, to another, using the available keypads or dials.

Digital pianos are often much simpler instruments, emphasizing quality of sound over feature-laden operation. However, some of the more sophisticated (and expensive) models combine the control features of portable instruments with the high-end samples typical of digital pianos. These too should be "test-driven" as much as possible in the store.

How many keys does the keyboard have?

Most portables have five-octave, sixty-one key keyboards. Most digital pianos have full eighty-eight key actions, like their acoustic counterparts, though some leave off a half octave at each end for a slightly more compact seventy-six note keyboard.

How many onboard sounds does the keyboard offer?

Many home portables don't accept new waveforms from memory cards or disks. The sounds you get are what you will have forever. Portable keyboards can be expected to come equipped with fifty to two hundred sounds. Digital pianos sometimes have many fewer, because high-quality piano samples require a good deal of memory; you're trading a wealth of sounds for a few very persuasive ones. There can be as few as five onboard sounds, or there can be over a hundred on the more expensive digital pianos with massive internal memories.

How many preset accompaniment patterns does the keyboard have?

Here again, the number of accompaniment patterns is often not expandable on the portables, so for variety's sake it is good to start out with lots of accompaniments. Expect to see between twenty and one hundred.

What are the keyboard's autoplay functions?

If automatic playing features are implemented on the keyboard at all, they will at least provide a preset rhythmic and harmonic accompaniment for your melodies. A few other features are basic. Usually you can set the key of the accompaniment by pressing a single left-hand note; this is called single-finger chord playing. If you're accustomed to playing your own chords, a setting called fingered chords should be present, allowing you to play basic chords that are then integrated into the accompaniment pattern, in whatever musical style you've selected. A synchro-start option enables you to trigger the beginning of the accompaniment by pressing any key on the keyboard, so you don't need to take a hand away to reach for the start button.

Also look for controls that access variations in the basic rhythm patterns. For example, if you're using the swing-jazz accompaniment setting, pressing a button marked Variation 1 (or something similar) will give you a different pattern but in the same style and tempo. Likewise, there might be buttons for introductions, endings, and rhythmic fills.

Is the keyboard velocity sensitive?

Velocity-sensitivity (responsiveness to different playing volumes) has become a very basic feature, but some of the less expensive units do not have it. For beginners, especially, it is almost as important a feature as weighted keys. Virtually all digital pianos have this feature.

Does the keyboard have a sequencer?

Home keyboards can encourage a beginner's first steps in composition and recording. The sequencers on some of the portables can be quite rudimentary, perhaps only recording sequences of preset patterns. But, for many people, anything more would be uninteresting and unused. Usually there are no editing features whatsoever, nor any ability to store sequences externally.

However, at the upper end of the portable keyboard market, some models have powerful sixteen-track sequencing capacity with a range of editing features. They are of course much more expensive, and when considering such an instrument you need to weigh the alternative of investing in a keyboard and sequencer as separate components. Still, there's no denying the convenience of having good sounds, flexible recording, and external storage in one highly portable keyboard.

How much does the keyboard weigh?

When it comes to home keyboards, some are much more portable than others! Even among the avowed portable models, there is a weight range of between six and fifty pounds. Digital pianos are much heavier, weighing between sixty and 280 pounds. The portable digital pianos are in the middle, ranging from twenty to ninety pounds.

Does the keyboard offer onboard effects?

Digital effects can do wonders for adding depth and spaciousness to any keyboard's sound. A little reverb adds an extra dimension to a piano sample, fleshing out the inherent inadequacies of a sampled timbre. It is especially welcome in smaller keyboards that have lower-grade samples and that play their sound through small speakers. But even larger digital pianos benefit enormously from digital enhancement.

Reverb is the most common effect, and if there is only one effect, it will be reverb. Sometimes you are offered a choice of a few reverb settings that imitate the reflective ambience of rooms and concert halls.

Does the keyboard come with the necessary peripherals?

It's surprising how often the answer is no. In particular, be sure that the keyboard comes with a power adapter. You may have to buy this at extra cost. Is the keyboard equipped with a stand for holding music? How about a stand for holding the keyboard itself? This last is usually not part of the price, because some people would just as soon put a portable model on a table. Digital pianos generally come with integrated stands, which are part of the furniture of the instrument.

While you're at it, check to make sure a sustain pedal is included.

Does the keyboard accept external samples and rhythms?

For keyboards that cost under about $1,000, the answer will usually be negative. These instruments are not expandable, and if the day should come when you tire of the factory sounds, and simply must have something new, your only option will be to buy a new instrument. If you think you might be getting into MIDI for the long haul, perhaps it would make sense to invest first in a keyboard with an open, expandable architecture.

Many of the top-of-the-line digital pianos accept sound cards or floppy disks loaded with new samples and/or new accompaniment patterns. These are usually manufactured by the same company that built the instrument.

If the keyboard has both a sequencer and a disk drive, find out whether it understands Standard MIDI File (SMF) format sequences. This is a universal standard with which sequences can be saved, filed, and then loaded into another sequencer for playback. (It is analogous to a computer text document that has been saved in ASCII format.) Surprisingly, not all keyboard sequencers understand this standard, preferring instead to deal only with their own proprietary files. The advantage to having a SMF-compatible sequencer lies in being able to share compositions with friends and acquire sequence files from third-party vendors and online services.

Does the keyboard offer external storage?

The attitude of most keyboard manufacturers seems clear: if the onboard sequencer is good enough to make music of any value, some means of saving that music will be included. In other words, the less-expensive instruments with rudimentary sequencers also save money by not having disk drives or RAM card slots.

Is the keyboard multitimbral?

Keep in mind that even if you decide not to get a model with a sequencer built in, the time may come when you will want to explore MIDI recording more. If the keyboard is multitimbral, all you will need to add to your setup is a sequencer. If not, you might need to also invest in an additional tone module, or a new integrated keyboard sequencer.

Many digital pianos are multitimbral even if they have no sequencer whatsoever, and they can be used effectively with an external data recorder.

25

General
MIDI Modules

Product Profile

General MIDI (GM) instruments represent the newest category of MIDI components, and it is a category that appears, as of this writing, to be expanding. The
General MIDI specification is designed to overcome incompatibilities in the way
sounds are organized in different tone generators, and to standardize basic aspects
of all the various operating systems (see chapter 17 for a complete description of
General MIDI). As MIDI expands into multimedia presentations and the number
of new MIDI users choosing GM products increases, manufacturers will doubtless
be encouraged to develop more sophisticated GM instruments.

As this is being written, there are two main formats for General MIDI: tone
modules and sound cards for computers. In either case, you will still need a MIDI
keyboard to send controlling data either to the module or to the computer.

All GM units contain the same sound set—a list of sound types corresponding
to predetermined program numbers. The actual sounds differ from one instrument
to another. So while program #1 will always be acoustic piano, the actual samples
will, of course, vary from one company to another. However, GM models are by
definition more similar to each other than non-GM instruments are; as more GM
hardware is developed, greater differences will undoubtedly emerge. Some modules
contain more than the required sounds; others only include the "official" 128
patches. Some offer editable sound parameters; others do not, and the sounds you
get are the sounds you live with. Some models are meant to function only as GM

players; others are full-blown synthesizers with GM-readiness as an additional feature.

Currently, GM modules cost between $300 to $1,300. The used market has not, at this writing, developed substantially.

Summary of Shopping Questions

1. Do you want a module or a sound card?
2. How does the module sound?
3. Is the module limited to General MIDI?
4. How many outputs/inputs does the module offer?
5. Does the module have a computer interface?
6. Can the module's MIDI channels be switched off?
7. How many oscillators does the module have?
8. Can you edit the module's sounds?
9. Does the module offer digital effects?

Do you want a module or a sound card?

This question is only relevant if you own a computer and plan to integrate it into your MIDI activities. A sound card plugs into an expansion slot of your PC, and essentially turns your computer into a tone generator. You still need a MIDI interface so that the computer can receive MIDI data from your controlling keyboard.

Cards are advantageous because of their compactness. The main disadvantage is that they are not transferable among different computer platforms.

How does the module sound?

All GM instruments have the same types of sounds, but not the same sounds. The samples used will differ, as will the manufacturer's interpretation of the more loosely defined sound types included in the GM sound set. It's particularly important not to assume that all GM modules are of the same quality, just because of their sound-set compatibility. The best way to audition a module is to play a GM sequence through it, because that's what GM instruments are primarily designed to do. When listening to the onboard sounds individually, pay particular attention to the leads, pads, FXs, drums, and pianos. Do the module's interpretations of these sounds suit your tastes and needs?

Is the module limited to General MIDI?

In some cases, GM is a mode that can be entered into or not, depending on how you want to use the module. For all its convenience, General MIDI has limitations, and it can be preferable to use the module without being restricted to the GM sound set.

How many outputs/inputs does the module offer?

With any tone module or keyboard, the more outputs there are (above the standard pair of stereo jacks), the more mixing control you will have when playing back a sequence. This is only true, though, if you're using a multichannel mixer, and if the mixer has enough inputs to take advantage of all the module's outputs.

Some GM modules also include audio inputs. This can be a handy feature, because it allows you to plug another sound source (like a second MIDI module) into the back, and merge the output of both modules into the main stereo outputs. This is especially convenient if you don't have a multichannel mixer; in this case, the GM module acts as a kind of limited mixer.

Does the module have a computer interface?

Some GM modules have a special jack on the back that connects them directly to a computer, without any additional MIDI interface. This is a great feature for someone who already owns a computer, is interested in enjoying prerecorded MIDI sequences, and wants to keep the investment to a minimum. Keep in mind, however, that if you want to record your own sequences, you will need a MIDI keyboard and a MIDI interface to connect the keyboard with the computer. In that setup, there is little advantage to the GM module having a computer connection.

If the connection will be used, the MIDI jacks on the GM module can still function in the normal way. So additional modules (whether they are GM instruments or not) can be placed in a MIDI data chain by using the MIDI THRU jack (setting up this kind of system is described in section 3).

Can the module's MIDI channels be switched off?

This feature would be used in the same way that you might mute a sequencer track, so that its part will not play. When playing back a GM sequence through a GM module, there are a couple of ways in which it could be useful to disable a particular channel.

- You can create a "music-minus-one" sequence by turning off the piano part, for example, and playing your own part along with the sequence.
- If you are using a second tone module, you might want a certain MIDI channel to be played by a patch in that other module (perhaps it has a better piano sample than your GM module). By turning off the channel in the GM instrument, the part won't be doubled.

How many oscillators does the module have?

The General MIDI specification calls for every GM instrument to have a polyphony limit of at least twenty-four voices. However, it doesn't define exactly what a voice should consist of, in terms of the tone-generating software. This ambiguity is potentially troublesome because some modules (this is true for non-GM equipment as well) allow more than one oscillator to be used in a patch. When two or more oscillators contribute to a sound, the result is usually a richer tone. Now, when manufacturers list their instrument's polyphony in the specifications, they may list the number of oscillators, rather than the number of actual voices that can be sounded at once. So a supposedly twenty-four-voice polyphonic module, when all the voices are using two oscillators, may become a twelve-voice polyphonic module. If some, but not all, of the patches are using more than one oscillator, then the polyphony will vary.

When shopping, try to determine how many oscillators are actually present in the module.

Can you edit the module's sounds?

This may not be an important question for everybody. After all, the basic purpose of GM modules is to sound good without programming. Still, it may be useful to have control over basic editing functions, such as attack rate and release rate of sounds. When playing back a GM sequence that was created with a different GM instrument, the voices may not respond in exactly the same way on your unit. Making the sequence sound as good as possible is often a matter of tweaking the sounds a bit, and is worth the effort.

Does the module offer digital effects?

This refers to signal-processing effects such as reverb. Reverb, in fact, is the most important effect for most musical purposes, and a little of it goes a long way toward making instrument samples sound more natural.

Glossary

Acoustic instrument. An acoustic instrument produces sounds by means of a vibrating string, an air column, or other nonelectronic means.

Action. The keys and key mechanisms of a keyboard instrument are called the action. See also: **Weighted action**

ADC. See: **Analog-digital conversion**

Aftertouch. Aftertouch is a type of MIDI controller data generated by pressing down on a key that has already been played. Polyphonic aftertouch affects each one of a group of played notes independently. Channel aftertouch affects all played notes simultaneously and equally.

Alternate controller. MIDI instruments modeled on nonkeyboard instruments, such as MIDI drum pads, breath controllers, and MIDI guitars, are called alternate controllers because they don't conform to the standard piano keyboard.

Amplitude. Technically speaking, amplitude is one of the variables in the shape of a sound wave, referring to the height of the wave, as opposed to its frequency. Amplitude determines the volume (loudness) of the sound created by the wave. See also: **Frequency; Envelope**

Amplitude envelope. See: **Envelope**

Analog-digital conversion (ADC). ADC is the process by which recorded sound is translated into binary information. ADC is used in samplers and digital tape recorders to record sound waves as data. See also: **Digital-analog conversion**

Attack. Attack defines the first part of a sound. As a sound-programming term, attack refers to the first stage of an envelope. See also: **Decay; Envelope**

Audio input/output. An audio input allows an electronic piece of equipment to receive an audio signal from another source; an audio output allows for audio signals to be sent out from one electronic instrument to another. Commonly, MIDI instruments feature output jacks that allow them to send audio information to an amplifier, so that the sounds they are producing may be heard through speakers.

Autoplay. Autoplay is the built-in accompaniment feature of many home keyboards, consisting of rhythm patterns, chords, and bass lines. Autoplay functions are accessed by playing specific notes with the left hand. See also: **Home keyboards**

Bank. A bank is an organized collection of sound programs (usually between sixty-four and one hundred). Patch banks exist within keyboards and can also be stored on disks or RAM cards. Performance banks are collections of multitimbral voice setups.

Bit. A bit is the smallest item of binary data. Bits are like letters of an alphabet that combine to form words (bytes).

Bit rate. The bit rate is the degree of resolution with which a sound sample is recorded or played back. The bit rate and the sample rate are the two variables that determine the fidelity of a sample. See also: **Sample; Sample rate**

Byte. A byte is a digital "word" made up of bits.

Cassette interface. A cassette interface allows digital information to be transferred to cassette tape for storage, used by some (mostly older) sequencers and drum machines to save sequences, rhythm patterns, or drum setups.

Channel. See: **MIDI channel**

Channel aftertouch. See: **Aftertouch**

Computer program. A computer program is a set of data instructions that allows you to perform a task on a computer. Computer programs are the software that stand between you and a computer, enabling you to give commands and receive responses. Computer programs are specialized to perform certain types of work and are loaded from a disk into the computer for use. See also: **Editor/librarian; Sequencer; Software**

Continuous controller. A device that generates a steady stream of MIDI data, as opposed to a single command, is called a continuous controller. Some examples are pitch-bend or modulation wheels, or breath controllers.

Controller. Within a keyboard, a device such as a pitch-bend wheel or sustain pedal that affects the production of sounds is called a controller. On the system level, a controller (often a keyboard) is used to send MIDI data out through a MIDI out jack to other devices, such as an external tone module, that are slaved to it. See: **Slave**

Damper pedal. See: **Sustain pedal**

Data recorder. See: **Sequencer**

Decay. Decay defines the last portion of a sound. As a sound-programming term, decay refers to the last portion of an envelope. See also: **Attack; Envelope**

Digital-analog conversion (DAC). DAC is the process by which a digital recording of a sound is translated into an analog signal. DAC is used in samplers and digital tape recorders to play back data as audible sound through an amplifier or other sound-reproducing equipment. See also: **Analog-digital conversion; Sample**

Digital audio tape (DAT). DAT tapes are small, cassette-sized cartridges that record sound digitally (rather than the standard analog cassettes) for higher fidelity.

Digital piano. A digital piano is an electronic keyboard instrument designed to emulate the sound of an acoustic piano through digital samples. Digital pianos usually have eighty-eight-key, weighted actions and integral stands, and offer other instrument samples in addition to piano sounds.

Digital signal processing (DSP). In a broad sense, DSP refers to any manipulation of a sound by means of a digital device. (A signal is simply sound being carried through wires, which has not yet been rendered in audible form by an amplifier and speakers.) There are many types of signal processors used in the production of music. Treating the sound signal with them is similar to processing a photographic negative in various ways before printing it. By artificial means, a more natural-sounding result is obtained. Common DSP effects are reverberation (reverb), digital delay (echo), and chorusing.

Drum machine. Drum machines are specialized sound modules designed to produce drum and percussion sounds. Most drum machines can be played by means of attached pads, have preset rhythm patterns, and are equipped with a sequencer for creating original patterns. See also: **Percussion module**

Drum pads. Drum pads are small buttons on drum machines that trigger the onboard drum samples. The term is also used for drumkit-style MIDI pad controllers used to trigger samples in any drum machine or percussion module.

DSP. See: **Digital signal processing**

Dynamic allocation. Dynamic allocation is one means by which voices are distributed among MIDI channels in a multitimbral setup. As opposed to fixed allocation, any MIDI channel can draw on as many voices as called for, within the limits of the instrument's polyphony. See also: **Fixed allocation**

Editing. Editing allows for the correction and manipulation of data. Sequence editing refers to changing the MIDI information in a recorded piece of music, and is performed on the levels of tracks, measures, or events. Patch editing refers to sound programming and involves changing the parameter settings that control what a patch sounds like. See also: **Editor/librarian; Sequencer**

Editor/librarian (Ed/lib). Ed/lib programs allow for the creation and storage of sounds. Most ed/libs are written for specific keyboards or tone modules, and provide a computing environment in which all the sound parameters can be easily viewed and adjusted. See also: **Computer program; Editing; Software**

Effects. See: **Digital signal processing**

Engine. A keyboard's entire voice-generating software and circuitry is called its engine. The term can be applied more generally to any computer processor.

Envelope. An envelope defines how a sound changes over time. In reality, as acoustic phenomena, envelopes change smoothly and are not broken down into segments. But, in synthesizers, envelopes cannot be perfectly smooth, so envelope generators operate in stages, defining attack, sustain, and decay. Synthetic envelopes can affect independently the volume (amplitude envelope), the tone (filter envelope), and the pitch (pitch envelope). The amplitude envelope makes a sound swell and fade; the filter envelope makes it brighter and duller; the pitch envelope makes it higher and lower. See also: **Attack; Decay**

Envelope generator. See: **Envelope**

Envelope stage. See: **Envelope**

Event. See: **MIDI event**

Expander. See: **Tone module**

Filter. A filter is used to eliminate or enhance a component of a sound. Usually, filters affect the frequency content, thereby changing the tonal quality. A high-pass filter eliminates frequencies below a certain setting; a low-pass filter eliminates frequencies above the cutoff point. Resonance filters emphasize the frequencies around the setpoint. MIDI data filters, as found in MIDI switchers, have nothing to do with sound. Instead, they eliminate or change a certain type of MIDI information, such as channel number or pitch bends, before passing the information further down the MIDI chain.

Filter envelope. See: **Envelope**

Fixed allocation. In a multitimbral setup, fixed-allocation systems allow for only one voice to be assigned to each MIDI channel. See also: **Dynamic allocation**

Floppy disk (Floppies). Floppy disks are magnetic storage media. Used in computers and some MIDI instruments, floppies are available in three sizes; 3.5-inch disks are the most common for music hardware. Floppies are flat and housed in a permanent case that is inserted into the disk drive

Frequency. Frequency defines the number of repetitions of a sound wave's shape per a specific time period; the more repetitions, the higher the frequency and the higher the pitch. See also: **Amplitude; Envelope; Filter**

Frequency shift keying (FSK). FSK is a synchronization time code that enables the timing of sequencers and drum machines to be controlled by a tape deck. Of all the time codes, FSK is the most awkward, because it can only be used when starting the tape from the beginning of a piece. See also: **Society of Motion Picture and Television Engineers; Song position pointer; Time code**

General MIDI (GM). General MIDI is a standard system to codify certain operations within MIDI instruments to make them more compatible with each other. This standard is implemented only in General MIDI (GM) equipment. The most noticeable feature is the GM sound set, assigning certain instrument types to specific program numbers. This enables one GM instrument to play back a sequence created by another GM instrument and produce comparable (if not identical) instrument sounds for all the parts.

Global settings. Global settings are parameters in a MIDI instrument that affect the instrument as a whole, such as tuning, transposition, and scale settings.

Hard drive. A hard disk drive works similarly to a floppy drive, but uses disks that are stiffer, permanently mounted, and hold much more information. As of this writing, a 3.5-inch floppy disk can store 1.4 megabytes of data, whereas many hard drives can hold hundreds of megabytes. Hard disks also transfer and access information much more quickly. Hard drives are sometimes built into samplers, or can be connected externally.

Hardware. A piece of electronic equipment, such as a keyboard, sequencer, or tone module, is called hardware, in contrast with the programs used to operate the equipment, known as software. See also: **Software**

Hardware sequencer. See: **Sequencer**

High-pass filter. See: **Filter**

Home keyboards. Home keyboards encompass a broad category of instruments including portables and digital pianos. These instruments can be used in professional settings as well, but are marketed for the recreational user. Many include auto-accompaniment features, and all have built-in speakers. See: **Autoplay; Digital piano**

Interface. An interface works between two incompatible operating systems, enabling them to communicate. MIDI is an interface between the various operating systems employed by digital instrument makers and computers. See also: **Operating system**

Keyboard tracking. Some keyboards offer the ability to change a sound's envelope according to where a note falls in the keyboard's range. For example, a sound could be made brighter as you move up the keyboard.

Keymap. A keymap is an arrangement of sounds assigned to specific keys of a keyboard. Keymaps are typically used with drum sounds to create a "drumset" of samples that can be played from a keyboard.

Kit. A kit refers to both an acoustic drumset and a collection of samples assigned to drum pads or a keyboard.

Linear sequencer. A linear sequencer is a data recorder that enables the user to record simultaneous tracks of varying lengths. See also: **Pattern sequencer**

Liquid crystal display (LCD). LCDs are the type of display screen found on most MIDI instruments and hardware sequencers.

Local on/off. The local on/off switch is a keyboard setting that disconnects the keys from the internal tone generator. When local off is set, the keyboard is usually being used to control external tone module(s).

Looping. Looping is the technique of extending the length of a short sample by causing it to repeat. Looping functions are included in the voice architecture of samplers.

Low frequency oscillator (LFO). An LFO creates vibrato and tremolo effects, the speed (how fast) and depth (how much the pitch varies) of which are usually programmable. LFOs are commonly found within keyboards or tone modules.

Low-pass filter. See: **Filter**

Megabyte. A megabyte is a unit of data storage equal to one million bytes. See also: **Byte**

Metronome. A metronome keeps time by audibly marking the beats of different tempos. Metronomes are incorporated into sequencers and drum machines.

MIDI cable. MIDI cables are specialized cords used to connect MIDI components to each other, through which MIDI data is transmitted.

MIDI channels. The sixteen subdivisions of all MIDI data through which all MIDI information, generated by a controller, is transmitted, are called channels. The receiving instrument must be set to the same channel if it is to respond to the MIDI data being sent over the cable.

MIDI component. Any hardware that sends and/or receives MIDI data.

MIDI event. A MIDI event is the smallest item of MIDI data, such as a note-on or note-off command. An event is a single byte of information, consisting of several bits. See also: **Bit; Byte; Note-on/note-off event**

MIDI interface. A MIDI interface is a device that connects MIDI equipment with most computers. The MIDI interface plugs into one of the computer ports, and translates MIDI data into a language understandable by the computer's operating system. Many MIDI interfaces also contain switching functions such as data merging and filtering.

MIDI jacks/ports. MIDI jacks or ports are electronic connectors found on the back of most MIDI equipment, into which MIDI cables are connected. The MIDI IN jack receives data from a controller; the MIDI OUT jack sends data from a controller; the MIDI THRU jack duplicates data received at the MIDI IN jack and passes it along to the next instrument in the MIDI chain.

MIDI merger. A merger has two MIDI IN jacks and one MIDI OUT jack. Its purpose is to merge the two incoming data streams into one outgoing stream, which can then be sent to a receiving instrument, or sequencer. See also: **MIDI switcher; THRU box**

MIDI retrofit. A retrofit takes an acoustic or non-MIDI electronic instrument and supplies it with MIDI controller capability, enabling it to receive and respond to MIDI data.

MIDI switcher. A device with multiple MIDI IN and OUT jacks to allow for various different routings of a system's MIDI data. Some switchers also are programmable, so certain setups can be programmed and stored for future use. A switcher is also known as a MIDI patchbay. See also: **MIDI merger; THRU box**

Mixer. A mixer receives several audio signals and combines them into a stereo output. The audio signals are fed into channels (not to be confused with MIDI channels), each of which can be adjusted for equalization, volume, pan position, and other aspects of the mix. See also: **Panning**

MS-DOS (Microsoft Disk Operating System). An operating system for IBM computers and so-called "clones."

Nonvolatile memory. Memory that is backed up by a battery pack so that it will not be destroyed when a piece of equipment is turned off is called nonvolatile. RAM is commonly nonvolatile.

Note-on/note-off event. These are MIDI commands generated when a key is pressed (on) or released (off).

OMNI mode. A setting that enables keyboards or tone modules to respond simultaneously to data on all MIDI channels. When an instrument is not in OMNI mode, it can be set to respond only to data on a single MIDI channel. See also: **MIDI channel**

Operating system. The internal software of a digital device that governs how it will work is known as its operating system. A synthesizer's operating system consists of its voice architecture, multitimbral capabilities, polyphony, and disk-storage routines. The operating system of a computer is the basic language that is spoken by all the software for that computer. Sometimes an operating system is called a computer's "platform." See also: **Computer program; Software**

Oscillator. Oscillators are the voice-generating circuitry in a keyboard or tone module.

Overdubbing. Overdubbing is a technique of recording a musical part on one track while listening to the parts that have already been recorded on other tracks. Originally referring to the ability to add parts to a stereo tape recording, the term is now also used to refer to the process of building up tracks in a sequencer.

Page. A subsection of a keyboard's program edit function. Each page will contain a group of related parameters.

Panning. Panning is used to adjust the stereo mix of a number of tracks. Mixers have a panning control for each input channel (also called a panpot), enabling you to move a single part from side to side in the stereo field by adjusting how much of the signal is delivered to each speaker. See also: **Mixer**

Parameter. In the broadest sense, a parameter is any adjustable setting. In keyboards and tone modules, parameters are aspects of a patch's sound that are changed when creating new sounds. A keyboard's voice architecture may contain several hundred sets of parameters. See also: **Page; Patch; Sound program**

Patch. A patch is a sound program consisting of parameter settings that are named and stored in MIDI instruments. Factory patches are the sounds that come loaded in a keyboard or tone module. See also: **Parameter; Sound program**

Pattern sequencer. A pattern sequencer is a data recorder that records information in repeated segments that may then be strung together in different ways to create a final piece. See also: **Linear sequencer**

Percussion module. A percussion module is designed to play mainly drum and percussion sounds. Unlike drum machines, percussion modules are usually rack-mounted and do not have drum pads. They are meant to be used with a keyboard controller in a sequencing setup. See also: **Drum machine; Drum pad**

Pitch-bend wheel. A pitch-bend wheel is a type of MIDI data controller that slides a note up or down in pitch. Usually, it is located at the left end of a keyboard. Sometimes, instead of a wheel, a small joystick is provided to create the same effect.

Pitch envelope. See: **Envelope**

Pitch modulate. See: **Low frequency oscillator**

Platform. See: **Operating system**

Polyphonic. Literally meaning "many-voiced," polyphony refers to an instrument's ability to play more than one note at a time. A piano is polyphonic, for example, but a flute is not. All MIDI instruments currently being made have some polyphonic capabilities; the limit to how many notes can be played at once is referred to as an instrument's polyphony.

Presets. The sound programs (patches) that come with a new keyboard are called presets (sometimes "factory presets").

Professional keyboard. A marketing category that denotes keyboards having advanced synthesis and controller features to offer better sound. Unlike home keyboards, professional models do not contain speakers and usually don't have autoplay features.

Program. See: **Computer program; Sound program**

Program change. A program-change command changes the sound being played by a keyboard or tone module. This command can be issued remotely, over MIDI, to change the patch of an external tone module from a keyboard or sequencer.

Programming. As a MIDI term, programming primarily refers to sound creation. To program a synthesizer is to make a new sound for it. It also refers to composing rhythm patterns in a drum machine, in which case it is called rhythm programming. Computer programming refers to the design and creation of software.

Programming hierarchy. Programming hierarchy defines the limits of a keyboard's ability to process waveforms. Also called the synthesis engine.

Pulses-per-quarter-note (ppq). Ppq refers to the number of subbeats that a piece of electronic equipment is capable of assigning to a quarter note. Each quarter note is further divided into a certain number of pulses (or time units) by a sequencer or drum machine. As ppq increases, so does the timing resolution of the instrument.

Quantizing. Quantizing automatically corrects timing irregularities. Notes (or any MIDI events) can be quantized to align with the value of quarter, eighth, sixteenth, or other note values through a sequencer editing command. Quantizing can often be applied with varying degrees of exactness, to avoid a mechanized rhythmic feeling.

Rack-mounted equipment. Box-shaped MIDI components, such as tone modules, that can be screwed into a standard nineteen-inch equipment holder, called a rack, are called rack mounted.

Rack space. The height of a standard rack slot—about one and three-quarter inches per space—taken up by rack-mounted modules. Most MIDI modules take between one and four rack spaces.

RAM/ROM cards. RAM/ROM cards are credit-card-sized memory cards that contain samples or voice data. When inserted into keyboards and tone modules, they expand the number of sounds that can be played by that instrument. RAM cards usually contain sound programs and can be erased and reused; ROM cards usually contain new samples and can be read but not erased. Random access memory (RAM). RAM is a memory chip that can be reused by erasing its contents and writing new data onto it. RAM is used to store original sound programs and multitimbral setups. In computers, RAM is used to run the programs being used and to hold temporary files created by those programs.

Release velocity. Release velocity measures the speed with which a key is let up as you remove your finger from it. Not all keyboards can measure release velocity. Those that can measure it use it to control different aspects of the sound. Typically, release velocity controls the rate of a note's decay, so that releasing a key quickly will cause a fast cutoff, while letting it up slowly will create a more lingering fade of the note.

Resonance filter. See: **Filter**

Reverberation (Reverb). Reverb is the reflection of sound waves in an enclosed space, such as an unfurnished room or a bathroom. As a digital signal processing (DSP) effect, reverb is created artificially and can be programmed to imitate different spaces, such as concert halls, small rooms, or caverns. It is the most commonly used DSP effect. See also: **Digital signal processing**

Read only memory (ROM). ROM chips can be read but not overwritten or erased. ROM is often used to hold factory samples in keyboards. In computers, the operating system is sometimes placed in the machine's ROM.

Sample. A sample is a digital sound recording. In the broadest sense, any digitization of a sound is a sample, even if it's an hour-long CD. Practically speaking, as a MIDI term, a sample is a short recording of an instrument playing a note, which is stored and played back across the range of a keyboard. The sample is created by taking audio "snapshots" of the waveform many thousands of times per second, and storing that data on RAM chips. In most cases, a single instrument sample actually consists of many samples taken at different points in the instrument's pitch range (this type of sample is called a multisample). This way, no single note has to be transposed too far when the keyboard is played; this is advantageous because transposing a sample usually changes its tonal quality. See also: **Analog-digital conversion; Bit rate; Digital-analog conversion; Sample rate; Sampler**

Sample Architecture. See: **Voice architecture**

Sample CD. A collection of instrument or sound effects samples recorded on CD for sampling. The individual samples are recorded by a sampler, and can then be played back using either the sampler's own keyboard or an external MIDI keyboard.

Sample-playback keyboard. This is a MIDI keyboard that uses factory digital samples as the basis of its sound programs. It can also be a tone module or drum machine.

Sample rate. During digital recording, the number of digital "snapshots" being taken of the sound wave per second is called the sample rate. The greater the sample rate, the more accurate the playback of the sample will be. Sounds that contain high frequencies require a high sample rate to be captured effectively. The sample rate is measured in kiloHertz (kHz); the sample rate for CD recording is 44.1 kHz (44,100 "snapshots" per second). See also: **Bit rate**

Sampler. A sampler is a MIDI component capable of recording sound digitally and playing it back through a keyboard. Some samplers are rack mounted and can be played from external MIDI keyboards. Samplers usually do not have any factory sounds installed in them, and can only play after a sample has been loaded into their memory.

Sequencer. A sequencer is a MIDI data recorder. Sequencers are usually, but not necessarily, multitrack recorders, enabling you to build complex musical arrangements part by part. Hardware sequencers are separate components, usually built in desktop style, as opposed to a rack-mounted design. Software sequencers are computer programs. In both cases, sequencers offer the same control over recorded musical data that computer word processors offer over text. Software sequencers are more graphically oriented and usually have more powerful features. Sequencers can also be found built into some keyboards.

Signal processing. See: **Digital signal processing.**

Slave. A MIDI component that is being controlled by a keyboard or sequencer is called a slave. Typically a tone module is slaved to a keyboard, but one keyboard can control another, and a sequencer can control any MIDI instrument. A sequencer can also be slaved to an external timing source, such as another sequencer or time code on tape.

Society of Motion Picture and Television Engineers (SMPTE). As a MIDI term, SMPTE (pronounced SIMP-tee) refers to a time code for synchronizing sequencers to videotape or audio decks.

Software. Software interfaces between the user and the computer's operating system, to perform some specialized task such as recording MIDI data or programming a synthesizer. See also: **Computer program; Hardware; Operating system**

Software sequencer. See: **Sequencer**

Song position pointer (SPP). SPP is a type of time code used for synchronizing sequencers with audio tape decks.

Sound card. A sound card is a tone generator printed on a circuit card, which is installed in a card slot of a computer. This effectively integrates a tone module into the computer.

Sound program. A sound program consists of a set of parameters designed to produce a certain tone; also known as a program or patch. Keyboards and tone modules (except samplers) come equipped with a collection of sound programs, as well as empty memory spaces for storing original ones.

Split keyboard. A split keyboard is divided so that different sounds are triggered from different portions of the keyboard. One example would have the left hand playing a bass sound while the right hand plays a piano sound. Some keyboards can be split into more than two parts.

Split point. On a split keyboard, the point at which one sound changes into another.

Standard MIDI File (SMF). SMF is a universal format for saving recorded sequences. These sequences can be loaded into any sequencer that recognizes SMF (most do). SMF is analogous to the ASCII format in computers.

Step entry. Step entry is the process of recording notes into a sequencer outside of "real time." Notes can be entered one by one, without regard to the speed at which they will eventually be played back.

Sustain pedal. On a piano, the farthest right of the three floor pedals is called the sustain pedal. It lifts the dampers off the strings, allowing notes to sustain (continue to sound) after the keys have been released. On MIDI keyboards, sustain pedals perform the same function digitally, generating MIDI data that can be recorded by a sequencer. They are also called damper pedals.

Synthesis engine. See: **Program hierarchy**

Synthesizer. A synthesizer is a digital instrument that can create new sounds from stored waveforms. Originally, "synths" used synthetic waveforms, such as sine and square waves, to create new sounds; in recent years, it has been common to also used sampled waveforms from acoustic instruments.

System exclusive (Sysex). The non-MIDI data generated by a digital instrument that it uses for its own internal processing is called system-exclusive information. This includes voice-architecture parameters, global settings, and the storage banks of sounds and multitimbral setups. Sysex data cannot be understood by instruments made by another manufacturer. See also:
System-exclusive dump

System-exclusive dump. A dump is the procedure by which system-exclusive information is transferred from one device to another. For example, the sysex settings of an instrument can be stored on a computer disk, to be reloaded later.

THRU box. A MIDI patchbay containing one MIDI IN and multiple MIDI THRU jacks is called a THRU box. Its purpose is to send a single data stream from a controller to at least two slaves simultaneously. See also: **MIDI merger; MIDI switcher**

Timbre. Timbre defines the tonal qualities of a sound. It is easy to confuse timbre with voice. A voice is a note, and several notes can be of the same timbre. In the MIDI world, different timbres refer to different patches or sound programs. See also: **Multitimbral; Voice**

Time code. Time code is an audio code that contains timing information and that, when translated into MIDI data by a converter, can control the timing of a sequencer. There are several kinds of time code, and they are used for synchronizing a MIDI recording with audio- or videotape. See also: **Frequency shift keying; Song position pointer; Society of Motion Picture and Television Engineers**

Timing resolution. The number of subbeats or "clocks" contained in every beat of a sequencer's metronome.

Tone generator. See: **Tone module**

Tone module. A tone module is a MIDI instrument with no controller features designed to produce different tones. Tone modules are either rack-mounted or desktop devices that are connected to keyboards and sequencers via MIDI cables. They include synthesizers, samplers, sample-playback instruments, and drum machines. Strictly speaking, a keyboard can be considered a tone module as well, simply on the basis that it produces tones.

Touch-sensitive. See: **Velocity-sensitive**

Tweak. Tweaking involves making small changes to a keyboard's preset sound patches.

Unweighted action. See: **Weighted action**

Velocity. The force with which a key is played on a MIDI keyboard, measured as the speed with which it travels downward while being struck, is called the velocity. This measurement determines how loud a note will be sounded. A keyboard whose loudness is responsive to the force with which its keys are pressed is called velocity sensitive.

Voice. A voice is a tone generated by a MIDI keyboard, tone module, or drum machine.

Voice architecture. In a MIDI instrument, the voice architecture is defined by the available parameters that can create or alter sound programs.

Waveform. A digital representation of a sound is called a waveform. When a sound wave is recorded digitally, it is translated into digital information that can be stored and used in the keyboard's patches.

Weighted action. A keyboard whose keys offer a slight resistance when pressed, to emulate the feel of an acoustic piano, is said to have a weighted action.

Workstation. A workstation is a single MIDI instrument that can perform several tasks. A typical workstation configuration is a keyboard with an internal tone generator, sequencer, and drum machine. Workstations are meant to be self-contained, music-production tools, with the ability to record and play back multitrack compositions.

Magazines

Music magazines have changed drastically in the last decade, reflecting the technological changes that have swept through the music world. Publications once devoted to acoustic instruments and music transcriptions now are filled with equipment and software reviews, as well as articles on how to get the most out of a home studio. They are a tremendous educational resource, and subscribing to one or more of them is highly recommended. The following periodicals deal mostly with keyboard-related music production; magazines with a focus on other instruments can be found at a good newsstand.

Keyboard
20085 Stevens Creek Blvd.
Cupertino, CA 95014

Electronic Musician
6400 Hollis St. #12
Emeryville, CA 94608

Mix
6400 Hollis St. #12
Emeryville, CA 94608

EQ
P.S.N. Publications
2 Park Ave.
Suite 1820
New York, NY 10016

Home and Studio Recording
22024 Lassen St.
Suite 118
Chatsworth, CA 91311

Pro Sound News
2 Park Ave.
Suite 1820
New York, NY 10016

Software Houses

Music software companies are in a very competitive business, and survival usually requires diversification. This means that most companies will produce software for more than one kind of computer, and also will develop more than one kind of software. A typical thriving software house will offer, for example, a professional sequencer, entry-level sequencer, a notation program, and several editor/librarians—and each program might be available for three different computer platforms. Because of this diversification, organizing a list of companies by category is difficult; there is too much overlap.

The following is a list of some of the more well-known producers of music software. It is not comprehensive and is not meant to imply any endorsements. Like any other individual, I am only familiar with the handful of programs I use regularly. In addition to using this list, check the advertisements and software reviews in music magazines. Also, many companies offer demo versions of their programs. These can be obtained through the mail or via downloading from a commercial online service.

BIG NOISE SOFTWARE
PO Box 23740
Jacksonville, FL 32241
Sequencing, librarian, and MIDI mixing software for IBM.

CODA MUSIC SOFTWARE
(800) 843-2066
Notation and other software for IBM/Mac.

EMAGIC
(800) 553-5151
Sequencing and notation for Atari/Mac.

MARK OF THE UNICORN
1280 Massachusetts Ave.
Cambridge, MA 02138
(617) 576-2760
Sequencing software and interface hardware for Mac.

OKTAL
315 Rene-Levesque East Blvd.
Suite 110
Montreal, Quebec
Canada H2X 3P3
(514) 844-3428
Sequencing for Atari/IBM/Mac.

OPCODE SYSTEMS
3950 Fabian Way
Suite 100
Palo Alto, CA 94303
(415) 856-3333
Sequencing and other software, interface hardware for Mac.

PASSPORT
100 Stone Pine Rd.
Half Moon Bay, CA 94019
(415) 726-0280
Sequencing, notation, and other software for IBM/Mac.

PG MUSIC
266 Elmwood Ave.
Unit 111
Buffalo, NY 14222
(800) 268-6272
Sequencing and other software for IBM/Mac/Atari.

STEINBERG-JONES
17700 Raymer St.
Suite 1001
Northridge, CA 91325
(818) 993-4091
Sequencing, notation, digital audio for IBM/Mac/Atari.

TWELVE TONE SYSTEMS
PO Box 760
Watertown, MA 02272
(800) 234-1171
Sequencing software for IBM.

VOYETRA
333 Fifth Ave.
Pelham, NY 10803
(914) 738-6946
Software and interface hardware for IBM.

Index